THE ROAD TO LONDON

Companion to this volume:

The Death Room:
Strange and Startling Stories
by Edgar Wallace

THE ROAD TO LONDON

EDGAR WALLACE

Edited by
Jack Adrian

WILLIAM KIMBER · LONDON

First published in 1986 by
WILLIAM KIMBER & CO. LIMITED
100 Jermyn Street, London SW1Y 6EE

ISBN 0 7183 0592 2

Photoset in North Wales by
Derek Doyle & Associates, Mold, Clwyd
and printed in Great Britain by
Biddles Limited, Guildford, Surrey

Contents

The Road to London was originally serialised
in the *New Magazine* for September, October
and November 1926. This is its first
appearance in bookform.

Introduction

The Road to London was originally serialised in three long instalments in the *New Magazine* in the autumn of 1926 – a time when Edgar Wallace was the most celebrated thriller-writer in Great Britain.

It's first-rate Wallace: there is a rich and beautiful heroine whose fortune is in imminent danger of being plundered; there is a murderous guardian whose financial empire is teetering on the edge of ruin; there is a mysterious and hideously-disfigured young man who is clearly not all he seems to be. There are two homicidal gangsters imported from Chicago, one of whom is appallingly proficient with a knife; there is a monstrous old lady who's as mad as a hatter; there is a crazed old wreck of a man whose feverish babblings may hide a terrible secret; and there is a chase – a frantic, headlong chase that hurtles through the Home Counties with heroine and hero ever on the verge of capture and death, ever just managing to evade their pursuers by the skin of their teeth only to be tumbled into yet another hair-raising and perilous situation. It is Wallace at his break-neck best, containing a rich mix of all the favourite ingredients with which he brewed up his most successful and enduring thrillers, and which turned him into the most popular and widely-read writer of his generation and beyond.

And yet, not only has *The Road to London* never been published in bookform, but, up until a few years ago, no one even knew it existed.

I stumbled across the story by chance – a copy of the issue of the *New Magazine* for September 1926, which carried the first instalment, picked up for pence in a junkshop – and after a brief run-through it was at once clear that here was something extraordinary. The instalment was roughly 23,000 words long and a note at the end promised another two parts, which meant that the full story must run to at least 60,000 words. And as none of the opening episodes was at all familiar, this in turn meant that here was what appeared to be a lost full-length Wallace thriller.

To be sure, with any prolific writer of popular fiction there is always the chance that something may slip through the net, and in the case of Edgar Wallace chance becomes a certainty. He not only wrote a huge number of novels, but a vast quantity of short stories – and certainly a good deal of his shorter fiction was never published in bookform, either in hard or soft covers. Publishers simply could not keep up with his prodigious output, and in any case Wallace's affairs were in such a chronic state of chaos for most of the time that even he lost track of his own material.

In 1920 he signed up with the literary agent A.P. Watt who managed to bring a certain amount of order into his life, as well as substantially increase his income by the simple expedient of forcing him to sign contracts with publishers which included a clause that guaranteed royalty payments on each book sold. Prior to this most of his novels were sold to publishers on an all-rights basis, often for as little as £70 a time. It's a sobering thought that, immensely wealthy as he became during the 1920s, Wallace's income could well have been doubled, for due to his careless way with contracts he never gained a penny royalty from many of his most famous books – including such super-sellers as *The Four Just Men* and *Sanders of the River*. On the other hand to Wallace the serial fee – the money he received from selling his novels to magazines and newspapers – was the chief object of the exercise of writing, and selling the serial to a book publisher afterwards was merely icing on the cake.

The impression one gets from the various biographies is that his period of greatest productivity began around 1925 and lasted until he died in Hollywood in 1932. But that was all part of the Wallace myth, the idea fostered by his main publisher, the canny Sir Ernest Hodder-Williams, that everything issued in bookform at any given time was fresh-minted almost that very month. It gave rise to jokes about the 'weekly' Wallace or the 'midday' Wallace, and the famous story of the man who rang him up to be told by a secretary to hang on as Wallace was only writing a serial. It was splendid publicity.

However a good proportion of the work published during the latter half of the 1920s had actually been written much earlier, and in fact Wallace was at his busiest during and just after the First World War.

During these years he edited and wrote copiously for the weekly *Town Topics*, produced reams of War commentary and propaganda, contributed numerous serials to a major provincial newspaper syndicate, prepared whole shelvesful of books for publication (in between August 1914 and November 1918 alone Wallace had around 40 published, of one kind or another), kept up a steady flow of short stories for a wide variety of monthly magazines, dashed off any amount of comic and dramatic monologues, sketches and playlets for the multitude of rapid-fire revues in London's theatres and music-halls, and churned out staggering quantities of cheap fiction and faction for the rapidly-expanding Dundee-based newspaper empire of D.C. Thomson.

For much of the time after Wallace's death it was assumed that he had not been a man to hide his light under a pseudonym and that virtually all his work appeared under his own name. There were, to be sure, three serials and one or two articles published under the byline 'Richard Cloud', but these were thought to be odd but minor aberrations. Only within the past ten years has it been found, by Wallace enthusiast John Hogan, that a positive embarrassment of pseudonyms peppers the pages of the newspapers and Sunday Supplements owned by D.C. Thomson (including John Anstruther, Arthur W. Frazer, E. Graham Smith and John Macey Dixon). Again, it was known that Wallace in 1913 had ghosted the memoirs of Evelyn Thaw, the chorus girl who had married the unhinged

American millionaire Harry K. Thaw who had subsequently murdered her lover. The memoirs had been serialised in the *Daily Sketch*, but it was only fairly recently that it was established that they had also been published in bookform, in 1914, adding one more title to the Wallace canon.

The present writer himself has not only added yet another pseudonym – Richard Freeman – to the lengthening list, but has also had the rare shock of discovering, only this year, a previously unrecorded book entitled *The Shell-man*: a non-fiction paperback about arms manufacture published in 1919. Even though this was issued under Wallace's own name, it has still lain lost and entirely forgotten for well over 60 years.

It's perfectly clear that the full extent of Wallace's prodigious output will never be known. A good deal of what he wrote, espescially during this period, was for hard cash, often handed across the editorial desk. Records, if they were kept at all, were minimal, and in any case many publishers' files were destroyed in the devastating fire-bomb raids of the Second World War; as was a high proportion of the bound volumes and single issues held by the British Library for copyright purposes.

Yet even so this still does not explain why a novel-length story serialised and – from its style – clearly written at the height of Wallace's fame should have vanished without trace almost as soon as it appeared.

The *New Magazine*, in which the novel appeared, was one of a stable of fiction magazines owned by the publishers Cassell, which included the *Corner, Cassell's Magazine, Argosy,* and the *Storyteller*. Like a good many of the monthlies it began life in the 1900s, an eager competitor in a field where George Newnes' prestigious *Strand Magazine* was the undoubted leader. Its page-count ran to 150, although on average thirty of those pages were taken up with advertisements, and another ten with illustrations to the stories. This still left 110 pages of text, which contained roughly 100,000 words of story-matter – and as there were another fifteen or so all-fiction magazines, as well as twenty or more periodicals with in between a third and two-thirds of their contents devoted to stories and serials, one may arrive at the staggering figure of over two million words of fiction published a month, every month, during the 1920s alone.

Many of the popular writers of the inter-War years had appeared in the pages of the *New* at one time or another: Sapper, A.M. Burrage, A.E.W. Mason, Frank H. Shaw, Baroness Orczy, Roland Pertwee, Talbot Mundy. Sax Rohmer had contributed a stream of short stories and serials, including his notorious *Dope* (1919), a thinly fictionalised version of the Billie Carleton cocaine-overdose scandal (the serial started within a few weeks of the end of the trial of the actress's supplier Reggie de Veulle although Rohmer, somewhat ingenuously, denied any connection).

From 1926 onwards, the majority of Wallace's own major thrillers were serialised in newspapers; only they could afford the huge fees that Wallace was now able, through his agent, to command. Certainly one or two did appear first in the monthlies, but this was due to Wallace's stout loyalty to Fleet Street's magazine editors who'd seen him through the bad times. Under the Old Pals' Act he was happy to let the *Grand Magazine*, for instance, serialise in 1926 his J.G. Reeder thriller *Terror Keep* (he had, after all, been writing for the *Grand* since 1908), and the editor was more than happy to make the biggest splash out of his good fortune that he could – *Magnificent New Mystery Story by the Author of 'The Ringer'!* bawled the adverts.

One might have thought that the editor of the *New* would similarly have pulled out all the stops to promote *The Road To London*. But he didn't.

Announcements of the serial were not so much low-key as almost no key at all, comprising just a few muted lines in the issue that preceded the first instalment. At the top of the front cover of the September issue itself appeared the line 'Brilliant Mystery Novel by Edgar Wallace', although without naming it and in lettering that was far from obtrusive and by no means exclamatory. The magic words 'new' or 'original' or 'exclusive' were noticeable by their absence. The rest of the cover was taken up with a scene from a short story by John Hunter, a more than competent and fairly prolific British pulp-writer who, at the same time, was to Wallace as a mouse is to an elephant. The story itself was crammed into three issues by using a very small type-face; this too was unusual. The next serial after Wallace's was *The Small Bachelor* by P.G. Wodehouse who by 1926 was still a relatively minor name: a mere writer of comic novels rather than the humorist of some genius as he was to be hailed from the 1930s onwards. Nevertheless, *The Small Bachelor* was trumpeted well in advance and ran over eight issues in a type-face that was definitely easy on the eye.

Which all seems very odd – until one starts digging beneath the surface, not only of the story itself but also its creation. For while a rough reading of the novel showed it to be an original, a closer analysis revealed that it bore a certain resemblance to another Wallace thriller, *The Northing Tramp*.

In *The Northing Tramp* hero and heroine are pursued by two murderous gunmen across upstate New York towards the Canadian border. They encounter numerous perils on the way but finally reach safety on the far side of the St Lawrence, where the hero discloses that he is in fact a rich English earl who made a bet with a villainous aunt that he could tramp from Washington DC to Canada without anyone discovering his identity. This suits the aunt who hires the gunmen to kill him so that his considerable fortune will then go to his next-of-kin, who just happens to be her son. In *The Road To London* the chase extends across the Home Counties, there is no aunt, and the hero …

But that is anticipating. To disclose what or who or why would spoil a rattling good yarn, for although the two stories have strong similarities (indeed, there are stretches of dialogue and descriptive matter which are identical to both), *The Road To London* is no mere rehash. Apart from anything else it is longer, and in fact it's now clear that it is *The Northing Tramp* which is the rehash and *The Road To London* the splendid original, for even though the records have been lost after so many years research has revealed a probable explanation of the whole curious business.

Wallace wrote *The Road To London* which was offered, like most of his work, to America for serialisation. For one reason or another the story was turned down. Perhaps it was considered too parochial; perhaps it was pointed out that while American readers were greedy for tales of foggy London and Scotland Yard (true, in those pre-Dashiell Hammett days), they might well be mystified by chases around rural England; possibly it was suggested that as he had a 'tramp' hero it might be a better idea to shift the locale across the Atlantic where the hobo theme was a popular one.

Although initially he had a short way with British editors who disagreed him that a story was 'the best I've ever written' (Wallace's invariable comment when handing something in), he was always happy to bow to American editorial pressure. The States paid better. Accordingly he rewrote to suit the American taste, in the process changing the location, dropping characters, chopping out sub-plots, and generally rendering down the storyline to its bare bones.

It was accepted, serialised, prepared for book publication. But he now had a 60,000-word thriller left on his hands which, though basically the same as *The Northing Tramp,* was at the same time radically different, certainly far more complex in its plot. Wallace had been in this kind of position before. In 1910 *The Nine Bears* had been published. The Americans hadn't liked that either, and he'd rewritten it to include an American hero. The result was issued in the States as *The Other Man* in 1911 but never published over here, although he'd subsequently used some of the new material in the construction of yet another thriller called *The Secret House* (1917). He was nothing if not resourceful.

However, he could hardly force his agent to push for *The Road To London* to be serialised in one of the major newspapers – who were all now clamouring for his work – because *The Northing Tramp* version was due to be issued as a book. Wallace hated waste, and 60,000 words was rather a lot of waste. What he needed was a periodical that would print the original story without making a vast amount of promotional fuss about it and, significantly, he chose the *New.*

At this time (1926) Cassells were preparing to jettison their magazine line and concentrate on book publishing. Circulations – especially of the *New* and the *Corner* – were by no means healthy, and it was too much trouble to try and revive them; within a year most of their periodicals would be sold off to the vast Amalgamated Press empire. For Wallace a moribund magazine was the ideal home for his redundant story, which was why the editor of the *New* was offered *The Road To London*, almost certainly at a low rate on the understanding that he didn't publicise it. Which, in turn, is why it sank without trace.

Until now.

Drastic literary surgery sometimes produces a finer creation. In this case nothing could be further from the truth. *The Northing Tramp* is but a shadow of its former self, for *The Road To London* is altogether the better story with its author at his most inventive, entertaining and thrilling. In a word, at his best.

Jack Adrian
August, 1985

Preface

Give a dog a bad name and hang him; give a woman a name which is neither Mary nor Jane, but hovers somewhere between the opposite ends of the poles, and she attracts to herself qualities and weaknesses which in some inevitable way are traceable to the misguided people who named her.

They who named October Jones were with the shades. There was only one of them had lived long enough to repent. October, under local and topical influences, had at various times and on particular occasions styled herself Doris Mabel and Mary Victoria and Gloria Wendy. At school she was Virginia Guinevere. She chose that name before she left home and had her baggage initialled 'V.G.J.'

'I'm afraid I can't get rid of the Joneses,' she said thoughtfully, her disapproving eye upon the J. 'That old man of the sea will hang around with his chubby little knees under my ears until I'm dead.'

'Or married,' said her parent wearily.

He had been a tall man, hollow-cheeked, long-bearded. Children did not interest him. October bored him. His wife, in those days something of a social butterfly, he seldom saw. Moreover, October had a trick of borrowing rare volumes from his library and leaving them on the damp grass of the lawn, or wherever she happened to be when it started raining.

'Jones is a miserable kind of name,' she suggested. 'Can't you change it, daddy?'

Mr Jones had sighed, and tapped his nose with a tortoiseshell paper-knife.

'It satisfied my father, my grandfather and my great-grandfather, and innumerable ancestors before them – '

Her brows knit.

'Who was the first Jones?' she demanded. 'I suppose they came out of their protoplasm simultaneous – '

' "ly," ' murmured Mr Jones. 'I wish you would get out of that habit, October.'

October groaned.

'What's the matter with Virginia?' she asked.

There was nothing that was October in her appearance, though October is a red and brown month. She was pinkish and whitish; she had April eyes, and her hair was harvest colour, when the corn is growing red. Nobody ever called her Virginia or Alys or Gloria Wendy or Guinevere, or anything but October. The nearest she came to an acceptable nickname was when somebody, reasoning along intelligent lines, called her 'Huit.' In another age she would have been a Joan of Arc. Lost causes had for her an attraction that she could not resist. She was by turns a Socialist, a Worker of the World, an Anarchist, and a Good Christian Woman. Cross October in the pursuit of her legitimate rainbows, and she was terrible. Thwart her, and you trebled her resolution. Forbid her, and she bared her feet for the red hot shares across which she was prepared to walk for her convictions.

Mr George Loamer, who was not greatly interested in women, young or old, accepted the guardianship which came to him on her mother's death without any idea of the complicated piece of mechanism he was taking in charge. In a sense he subdued her by his magnificent lack of comprehension. Her subtle sarcasms were wasted on a man whose subtlety was supplied by a mother of whom he stood in dread, and of whose existence October had not the slightest inkling, until one day when, crouched with a tramp behind certain bushes, she saw that eagle-faced woman pass. But that is anticipating.

This was Mary October Jones – she had acquired a 'Mary' in passing – who was one day to take the London road, hide under hedges, creep into deserted factories, her companion a disreputable tramp with a black eye.

As to Mr Loamer, her guardian ...

There is a department at Scotland Yard which deals with Curious Happenings. In a big room, the double-windows of which look across the Thames, sits a man who has no other business in life than to tabulate gossip. The by-products of fact that come into that gloomy building reach him and are noted. From the vast heaps of waste that are examined he sometimes extracts a few fine particles of golden truth which are often immensely valuable to the more prosaic branches of his profession.

Central Inspector Simpson strolled in one afternoon and found him poring over a grisly photograph which had come to him from an East London coroner's court.

'Pity that man Quilting had no friends or relations – got an idea this is the feller.'

'Quilting?'

'In List C – Missing.'

The inspector remembered.

'Queer coincidence – five – six people all in the same class. Men with money who have flutters on the market – no friends – all operated through Loamer's – all vanished.'

Simpson sucked at his pipe glumly.

'Loamer handles thousands of accounts. You're thinking of Dr Elvington? Loamer reported that himself.'

'In the past twenty years – ' began the patient collector of news.

'Nonsense! Loamer is a very rich man.'

'I wonder!' said the collector of gossip, who believed in nothing and nobody.

That same day Mr Simpson had an interview with the head of the City Police, and certain investigations were put in trim – a few days too late, as it proved, to save October Jones from a great deal of fear and discomfort, and Mr Nigel Black, that wealthy young man from New York, from several narrow escapes from death.

PART ONE

I

Just as there was something about Mr George Loamer that was wholly different from and superior to all other human beings, so there was something about his office which marked it as different from and superior to all the other offices in the City of London.

Mr George Loamer was unique in that he was not an individual obscuring his individuality behind a corporation, a company, or a syndicate. He was just himself, a name in dull gold letters on a grey stone facia without reservation or qualifying appendage.

The building occupied a very small plot in Lombard Street. It had four floors, on which his managers, cashiers, accountants and clerks worked in luxurious surroundings – areas of polished mahogany and plate glass enclosed within marble walls. Here they kept track of his multifarious transactions, his incursions into the rubber market and the rail market and mining market. For Mr George Loamer confessed himself good-humouredly as a gambler on the Stock Exchange, and there was such material proof of his prosperity that the word lost much of its disreputable meaning.

He was a very tall man, stout and broad-shouldered. His face was very red and good-humoured, and he smiled most of the time. His thin, sandy hair was brushed back from his high forehead, and he wore invariably a perfectly fitting frock coat; a double-breasted waistcoat, across which looped a heavy gold chain.

He was smiling one morning in late spring when a solitary sumach tree in the paved courtyard beneath his window was putting forth its new green, and his smile had the quality of benevolence. His companion was a small, shabby-looking woman in the early forties, with a lined, sad face and a nervous trick of pinching her bloodless lips. Her faded blue eyes were fixed on Mr Loamer in pathetic appeal.

She sat opposite Mr Loamer, fiddling with the ivory handle of an umbrella, and she was obviously ill at ease.

'My dear Miss Elvington,' said Mr George Loamer in his most comforting tone, 'nobody knows better than you how much I would give to learn your father was alive. May I suggest, as I have suggested year after year, that I am the last person in the world with whom he is likely to communicate.'

The faded woman stirred uneasily.

'My father was a very wealthy man – ' she began.

Mr Loamer closed his eyes wearily.

'Yes, yes' – his voice was little more than a murmur – 'I know – I know! And an eccentric man. I have always thought that Dr Marcus was a very eccentric man. I do not wish to hurt your feelings, but – er – I have thought that possibly his mind was a little ... shall we say ... affected?'

'He was strange but he wasn't mad,' she said with spirit. 'He drew a hundred thousand pounds from the bank – the proceeds of the sale of his properties – and was never seen again.'

Mr Loamer nodded. He was very patient. Once in every three months he had to endure such an interview as this: he was almost inured to the experience.

'I never saw him, my dear lady,' he said gently. 'When you reported his disappearance I was the first to inform the police. He was a client of mine. I certainly had made a little money for him, but at the time of his disappearance he owed me the best part of four thousand pounds. As I say, I should be the last person in the world he would communicate with. He told me the previous day that he was going abroad; that is all I know.'

He sighed, twiddled his short thumbs and looked appealingly at the ceiling. The little woman rose, gathered up her worn bag and umbrella.

'It is rather hard living in that big house alone,' she said. 'The expense is terrible.'

Mr Loamer did not suggest that she should sell the house. He had offered the suggestion before, and he was anxious to cut short the interview. Presently, he thought, she would tell him that she had a small income inherited from her mother. She always told him that. To his relief she said nothing more except to bid him a timid good-bye. He opened the door for her and watched her disappear into the gilded elevator, and, going back to his desk, sat down to await the arrival of Mr Nigel Black.

Nigel came swinging across the broad outer office on time; would have started his business then and there but for the fortuitous circumstance that, displaying the mysteries of his sanctum, Mr Loamer drew back a small panel and revealed a window which gave him an uninterrupted view of the outer office.

'I like to feel that I can, by pressing a button as it were, bring my staff – my more intimate staff – under observation.'

'By Jove!' said Mr Nigel Black, in wonder.

It was not the mechanism or the ingenuity which surprised him. Looking over the shoulder of the young man, Mr Loamer frowned, blinked and then smiled. If there was annoyance in the smile, he did not betray himself.

'My ward,' said he, a little grandly.

Nigel Black looked through that small observation window which afforded Mr Loamer a view of his outer office. 'My ward' was standing by the desk of the cashier, and he saw at first only the graceful lines of her and the back of a biscuit-coloured toque, for her face was turned from him. A tiny diamond glittered on the white finger of the hand that rested on the desk, and he wondered, as young men wonder almost mechanically, if she was engaged and to whom. He was never quite sure which was the engagement finger. Fair … he saw the dull gold of her hair over the ears. A very gracious figure. And then she turned her head. The profile was perfect – he guessed the splendour of her eyes. In profile her lips were full and red.

'My ward,' said Mr Loamer again, and as he spoke the girl turned from the desk and went slowly out of the room.

Nigel scratched his nose thoughtfully.

'What the devil are you doing with a ward?' he demanded, and Mr Loamer smiled complacently.

'Her mother, a widow, was a dear friend of mine, Mrs Hallaman Jones. Rich? Oh, yes. Hallaman Jones was – um – artistic – but rich. When he died his dear wife put her business in my hands. She was my best friend.'

'Dead?'

Mr Loamer nodded gravely.

'She died in my house rather suddenly. A heart attack four years ago. I was sole executor of her will.'

Nigel Black was not greatly interested in the late Mrs Jones; he thought the name was rather usual. In a second she had passed from his mind. The ward in the biscuit-coloured coat and the little toque was not so easily forgotten.

'She's certainly beautiful,' he said, and added: 'So far as I could see her.'

Here Mr George Loamer should have invited him to meet his ward, should have explained that she was curiously named after the russet month in which she was born, and added such spice of detail as would have piqued the curiosity of his visitor. There was every reason why he should, for Nigel Black was the type of young man that guardians dream about. He was very good-looking, very wholesome, an out-of-door man, and solidly rich. But for a motive that was good and sufficient he did not excite the curiosity of his visitor.

'Now let us talk business,' said Mr Loamer gravely, a trifle pompously.

There was business to be talked, for Nigel Black had arrived two days before from New York and the voyage had been punctuated by radio messages concerning the state of the rubber market.

Nigel Black had all the virtues of clean youth and most of the advantages which come to very rich young men. He had one gentle but ineradicable vice – the desire for adventure which is so often expressed in these humdrum and peaceful times on the floor of the Stock Exchange or that space verging the green ribbon of the turf where men speculate on the erratic qualities of the racehorse.

It was his misfortune that his gambling propensities produced a profit, otherwise he might have grown bored of folly and developed an interest in those gilt-edged securities; the movements of which so seldom raise a flutter in the most susceptible bosom. It was when rubber had dropped to an incredibly low level that he met Mr George Loamer in the grill room of the Astoria, for Mr Loamer was on one of his periodical visits to the United States, and when introduced, as he was, by an enthusiastic friend to 'one of the big men in London finance,' he accepted this extravagant estimate of Mr Loamer's stability.

Mr Loamer was not unknown on Wall Street. He was regarded as a 'safe' gambler who had built a huge fortune by the exercise of an admirable judgment not usual in speculators. He was a broker who acted for quite important people in America, but it was generally understood that his operations where of the more secret kind, that he was in fact a 'rigger,' who could manipulate stock to the advantage of clients who desired anonymity.

Mr Loamer talked 'rubber' in his soothing way, spoke easily of production, of plantations, of reserves. Here was rubber at thirteen cents a pound. It could not fall lower. All the world's traffic was carried on rubber – he had motor-car statistics at his finger tips.

Now suppose ... His gold pencil flew along the smooth white table cover – many a laundry hand had examined Mr Loamer's pencilled calculations without understanding them.

Nigel Black was fired with the plausibility, the logic of his new friend's calculations. He gave Mr Loamer a tentative commission then and there, and within a month found himself the richer by twenty thousand dollars.

And then Mr George Loamer had advanced the details of a great scheme that brought the young man to London and to the greatest adventure of all.

For two hours they sat in the guarded office, and then Mr Loamer rose stiffly, and locked away his documents in the big safe.

'Lunch,' he said peremptorily.

Outside in Lombard Street a man in rags was walking along the edge of the sidewalk, his eyes glued to the ground. Now and again he stooped and picked up a cigarette end from the gutter. Nigel was watching him curiously when Mr Loamer joined him.

'Shooting snipe!'

Nigel's white teeth showed in a grin of joy.

'Makes me feel homesick to see that hobo gathering in the sheaves,' he said.

Mr Loamer's interest was of the mild and disparaging kind.

'How these beasts live I can't imagine,' he said. 'A friend of mine in the police department told me that some of them cover Europe, and one, he knew, walked from London to Madrid and back in a year. That of course is a lie. Without a passport it would be impossible to leave the country – '

'Listen,' protested Nigel Black. 'You may be a whale of a financier, but human nature is a sealed book to you, Mr Loamer.'

And he proceeded to tell stories, and out of these stories grew one which Mr Loamer invented for himself.

II

Mr Loamer's car brought him to Kensington and to one of the broad avenues leading from the High Road. The Rolls stopped before the stone portico of a big corner house, and scarcely had his shining shoes touched the pavement when the door was opened by a footman. The financier strode into the hall, stopped before a mirror to arrange his cravat and smooth back a strand of hair that had come out of place. He brushed his coat, glanced at his hands a little anxiously, and mounted the broad stairway.

The room into which he was ushered was of magnificent proportions; the furniture old and costly. A priceless tapestry half covered one wall, the few pictures that glowed in the light of concealed lamps were veritable masters.

Though the day was warm, a small fire burnt in the big fireplace, before which sat a woman. She turned her head as he came in and her dark eyes surveyed him in an incurious stare. Her hair was a whitish-grey, the face sallow-pale, a pair of thin, bloodless lips and a huge hook nose were the striking features of her pinched face. About her neck were rope upon rope of pearls, a huge diamond sparkled in either ear, and it seemed that wherever jewels could be placed upon her person they had been pinned or hung. She glittered with every movement; her fingers were hardly visible for rings.

Mr Loamer came nervously towards his mother, raised her hand to his lips and kissed an emerald or two.

'Sit down, George.'

Meekly he sat on a low chair before her.

'You have seen the report of the Agar Syndicate?'

He nodded.

'Very unfortunate,' mused Mrs Loamer, 'but not irremediable. Without my advice you would of course be ruined. How much have you lost?'

'The greater part of a hundred thousand pounds,' said Mr Loamer huskily.

He did not protest that it was her idea to finance the fantastic scheme for mining rubies in a country which had never yet produced a ruby. He might look back across the wreckage of a score of schemes which she had propounded in her dominating way, and the past was littered with the debris of a dozen fortunes broken in the attempt to acquire easy money. The Sunken Treasure Scheme, the Cocos Island Expedition, the Sea Gold Syndicate – he could not think of them without wincing. But he made no comment.

She fingered her pointed chin thoughtfully.

'What exactly is the position, George?' she asked.

Mr Loamer cleared his throat.

'The Bank have called in the overdraft, and Waltons threaten to sue for their account.'

'How much is it?' she asked.

He mentioned a sum which would have staggered most

people – Mrs Loamer's eyes did not so much as blink.

'This wretched girl, October Jones – ?' Mr Loamer licked his lips.

'£143,000 18s 9d,' he said exactly, 'and it is her birthday next month.'

His mother looked up at him.

'Her birthday?'

He nodded.

'Twenty-one. I must give – um – an account of my stewardship.'

Her eyes narrowed.

'But I thought you said you hadn't touched that?'

'I can't touch it,' he said, a little glumly, 'until next month. There's a small sum – twenty thousand or so – involved in the securities which I have lodged against our overdraft, but the remainder is to all intents and purposes in Chancery. I merely administer the income.'

Mrs Loamer turned her gaze to the small fire, staring into its dull depths.

'I suppose the American did not come?' she said. 'That was bad management on your part, George.'

'He has come,' he interrupted her, 'and he has brought the money.'

She looked round quickly at this.

'All the money – the amount you suggested?'

He nodded.

'He has brought it in cash – dollar bills. I made that clear to him when I was in New York. You cannot operate in rubber without you have fluid capital. The money is deposited in my name at the Birmingham Bank.'

Their eyes met.

'I am bringing him to dinner to-morrow night, mother,' Mr Loamer went on nervously. 'He is a peculiar young man, but I think you will like him.'

'Peculiar?' She frowned. Mrs Loamer was something of the grand lady; she did not like peculiar men, young or old; they jarred with her stateliness.

'Not vulgar, I hope?' she suggested.

'No, no,' he hastened to assure her, 'certainly not vulgar. He is inclined to make extravagant bets. On the way to the Carlton he offered to bet me a thousand pounds that we should meet a green taxi driven by a man with a red moustache.'

'That savours certainly of vulgarity,' said Mrs Loamer icily.

She thought a little while.

'Yes, you may bring him to dinner. We will have the gold service, and I would like Cavalini to sing to us after dinner.'

Mr Loamer wriggled.

'He will charge two hundred, and I'm not certain that we can get him at such short notice,' he wailed.

Mrs Loamer's hand waved majestically.

'Don't be tiresome, George. Arrange this for me. And that new Polish violinist is in London – Bourjerliski. I should like to hear him. Lady Elmer told me that he played at the Duchess of Alton's party the other night, and his terms are quite moderate – a hundred and fifty, and twenty-five for the accompanist. Arrange this also, George.'

Mr Loamer sighed heavily and nodded.

'This October woman – we must do something about her. Is she pretty?'

George Loamer scratched his chin.

'I suppose she is. She's rather a nuisance. I'm sending her away on the Continent for three or four months – things may straighten out by then. Miss Elvington was in to-day.'

He said this with some significance; so terrified was he of this eagle-faced woman that he never made any direct revelation of thought, and in all their association had approached delicate matters obliquely.

'Miss Elvington?'

The old woman pursed her thin lips.

'Poor Marcus! I am sorry for him. But it was necessary. Let that be an example for you, George. I put aside all my own feelings, my own emotions, for the good of the House. It is unfortunate that we should have lost the money in an aeroplane invention introduced by that objectionable young man whose lies I will never forgive.'

Again he might have protested that the objectionable young

man had not been his friend, but hers.

She sat thinking, her chin on her palm, her eyes closed, and so fearful was he of interrupting her that he scarcely dared breathe. Presently the big eyes opened and transfixed him.

'When you were in America, I asked you to do something for me.'

He wriggled uncomfortably in his chair and did not answer.

'I have always been interested,' she went on slowly, 'in that type of desperado which certain cities of the United States seem to produce so prolifically,' She paused.

'I found two men,' he answered doggedly. 'I told you I found them. A State detective brought me in touch with them. But what use would they be to us? Don't you see, mother, you would be putting our lives in their hands?'

'Do you know their addresses?' she interrupted him.

He nodded mutely.

'Cable them money to come here,' she said. 'I have no doubt the American police will be glad to see the back of them.'

'But what use – ?'

'Cable them!' It was an order.

'October.' Mrs Loamer shook her head and frowned. 'I think you had better marry her,' she said astonishingly, and Mr Loamer staggered.

'Marry her?' he almost squeaked. 'But, my dear mother, she would not think of marrying me.' And then, with a sudden burst of almost hysterical fury: 'Can't we sell things? Can't you give up this place? It costs a fortune. Cavalini! We might be able to pull things out of the fire. I've got these three houses running and they are ruinous! And the risk ... suppose old Elvington's found, or other things come out ... ruin – imprisonment perhaps. Mother, I've always done what you wished. Always. You could have saved me a lot of worry. You should have looked after October ... she doesn't even know that you exist ... '

His voice graded down to a dismal plaint.

Mrs Loamer silenced him with an upraised hand.

'I see everything,' she said simply and majestically. 'George, you may go. Bring your friend to-morrow at half-past eight.

By the time you have returned I shall have had one of my Inspirations.'

It was a crushed and baffled man who crawled back into his car. He sat bunched up in one corner, his chin on his breast, his mind a confusion. This woman who planned so madly would be his ruin, his death. And yet he had lived in bondage to her all his life.

Long after the car had struck the open country road he was trying to collect his wild thoughts into a coherent stream.

The car swept up the broad drive of Market Chase. He saw a slim figure practising putts on the lawn. She turned her head as he descended from the car, and went on with her task. There was neither friendliness nor antagonism in the gaze that met his; rather a painful patience.

'Have you been back long, my dear?'

'An hour,' she said laconically, and swung her putter again.

'Milton brought you back all right? I saw you in the office.'

The clear, grave eyes met his.

'Milton took me to your office, where I cashed a cheque; he took me to Dover Street; he saw me carefully inside the car and brought me back.'

Mr Loamer forced a laugh.

'My dear, you go on as though he were your keeper,' he said. 'Why didn't you come and see me? That wasn't friendly, October.'

She sighed impatiently and faced him again.

'They told me you were terribly busy. I saw you peeping at me through your little spy-hole, and I felt rather as if I were being exhibited. Who was the other sightseer?'

Mr Loamer coughed.

'A young American, a fellow named Nigel Black – um – he thought you were pretty.'

'Do Americans think such things?' she asked with a half-smile.

There was an awkward pause here. Mr Loamer, taking the putter from her hand, was examining it curiously, as though he had never seen such an instrument before.

'In a few days, my dear October,' he said oracularly, 'the

world will be opening for you. New sights, new visions, new experiences will come to you. And I am wondering – um – whether you will enjoy your new-found freedom.'

'I'm wondering, too,' she said, her eyes twinkling.

'It is a grave responsibility for you, and not only for you, but for me. I suppose – um – marriage will come in the ordinary course of events, and I am wondering, October, indeed I am deeply concerned, whether it would not be better if you remained a little longer under my care until your mind matures, as it were. The world is full of fortune-hunting men, and the young girl is wise who chooses as a mate a man, let us say, of riper years and experience.'

She was looking at him steadily, but obviously she was thinking of something else. Her mind was miles away.'

'Nigel Black,' she said. 'That name seems almost familiar – he's an American millionaire, isn't he? Is he a friend of yours?'

'A very dear friend,' said Mr Loamer. He was not being untruthful from his point of view, for all friends of his were 'very dear friends.'

'I remember now,' she said presently. 'I read a book of his.'

Mr Loamer's mouth opened in an O of astonishment. He was totally unaware of his dear friend's literary achievements.

'Wait a moment!' She flew into the house, was gone a minute or two and, coming back to meet him in the hall with a book in her hand: 'It is he,' she said triumphantly. 'Look!'

He took the book from her and turned to the title page. It was called *The Hobo Student*, and the brief introduction told of a Yale scholar who had spent his vacation amongst the tramps of Western America, 'riding the rails and decking the fliers' with the best of the professionals.

'I'd love to meet him, Mr Loamer.'

'Uncle,' he murmured, but that invitation had never been accepted.

'Couldn't you bring him here? You've no idea how terribly dull it is at Market Chase. Perhaps,' she added wickedly, 'that might solve the problem of my marriage.'

Mr Loamer, who was a delicate man, winced at the crudity.

III

It was exactly four weeks and three days after Nigel Black dined with the great financier and his mother that Mary October Jones came to a decision. She could remember the date precisely, because it was on the eve of her twenty-first birthday. She was walking up and down the drawing-room at Market Chase, stopping now and again to look through the long windows to the lawn and the dark line of Havvick Wood beyond. The sun had gone down, but the lemon light of sunset tinted the darkening sky.

Twenty-one seemed a tremendous age: tomorrow a new life would begin, a life from which certain shadows would be lifted. Substantially the greatest shadow of all was cast by Mr George Loamer, but there were shades a little more terrifying. Mr Loamer had friends and associations gathered in the fifty-five years of his life. People whose names she scarcely knew. Newest and most terrifying of these were Red Beard, a stocky, silent man, and the fat man called Lenny, who she was sure was Italian. They had appeared most unexpectedly about ten days after she introduced Mr Loamer to that literary masterpiece *The Hobo Student*. She had been reading under the shade of a big oak one warm Sunday afternoon when they crossed the line of her vision. Mr Loamer was in his library writing letters.

A tall, thick-set man with a short red beard, and a fat little man whose face was broader than it was long, the breadth being emphasised by the straight black eyebrows and moustache. They were striding out side by side, the little man's head no higher than his companion's shoulder. They favoured October with a quick sidelong stare and marched up to her, keeping in step like soldiers.

'Mornin', miss,' said the tall man. 'I guess this is Market Chase – tha's what the ginty man said, Lenny?'

'Thasso,' grunted the little man.

She had risen by now and had recovered from her astonishment.

'I will tell Mr Loamer you're here,' she said.

'Friends from Chicago,' said Red Beard. 'Name of O'Flynn ... hardware.'

She walked to the house in time to see Mr Loamer hurrying out. He was a trifle breathless – but then, he had been that way for over a week. Nervous, irritable, ready to jump at any sound.

'Er – um – yes ... some friends of mine ... business friends from New York ... Mr ... Hennessy, and Mr ... I forget.'

He hustled them into the house. She did not see them leave, only Mr Loamer was more nervous than ever at dinner that night. She had seen them again. In the middle of the night the roar of a motor engine had wakened her and looking out in the moonlight, she saw Red Beard talking in low tones to Mr Loamer, who was in his dressing-gown and pyjamas.

There was something about Red Beard that frightened her. Why this should be so, she did not know. He was more furtive than the stout, oily-faced woman who made such mysterious appearances at the Chase.

Mr Loamer had not been to the office that day. At breakfast he had been abstracted and nervous. There were deep shadows under his eyes, and he had the haggard appearance of a man who had missed sleep. He had made a pitiful attempt at gaiety, had produced with a flourish the tickets for the Italian tour he had planned for her, and at the tail end of the breakfast, after a long succession of silences:

'October, my dear, there are certain documents to sign. They are coming down from town to-day – um – about your estate. You have, of course, no estate literally. You have money, but that is a legal term – '

'Mr Loamer,' she interrupted him, 'don't you think that I should have a lawyer at this stage?'

He forced a smile.

'A lawyer, my dear?' he said, almost jovially. 'My lawyer is looking after your interests. You need have no fear whatever. I will arrange everything for you – even your marriage settlement.' He coughed, and did not meet her eyes.

'My marriage settlement? But I am not thinking of getting married.'

'You will,' he said huskily. 'It is as certain as anything can be, that a beautiful girl like you will not be allowed to go single all your days. My mo – a friend of mine, one of the wisest, shrewdest, dearest creatures in the world, is very much interested in you, October. She suggests that you should marry a man of some – weight, let us say.'

'Avoirdupois?' asked October, a little cruelly. And it needed only his red face to tell her what was in his mind, and in spite of herself she laughed.

'But that isn't done, is it. Mr Loamer, excepts in books? I mean, the marriage of guardian and ward.'

In his confusion he had no answer to give. This was a very crude variation of the speech he had prepared.

'I think we ought to be very frank with one another, Mr Loamer.' She folded her serviette deliberately and thrust it into the enamelled ring. 'Since my dear mother died with such terrible suddenness, and you became my guardian, you have been very kind and sympathetic, but we have nothing in common. I am not thinking of your age: that really makes no difference,' she added quickly.

She had seen the colour go from his face and had misread the signal.

'I have been virtually a prisoner at Market Chase, haven't I? I know that's a terribly dramatic way of putting it, but it is very near the truth. You have given me the use of an electric runabout which cannot run more than twenty miles without recharging; you have never allowed me to go to town except with Milton, who has not let me out of his sight – in fact, you've not given me the slightest opportunity of meeting any other man than yourself.'

Mr Loamer's face went suddenly red again.

'I had no idea of keeping other men from you,' he protested explosively. 'Good God! I hadn't thought of myself in that connection until … anyway, I hadn't any idea of marrying you or any other woman.'

She knew he was speaking the truth.

Since breakfast she had not seen him. Somebody had arrived from London that afternoon: she guessed it was the messenger bringing the documents which she was to sign, and her resolve was that in no circumstances would she put pen to paper without independent advice. She was not alarmed; it was, she told herself, merely the new spirit of independence, the desire to break effectively with the restraining influences which had overshadowed her during the past years, that fostered this revolt. And when Milton, who was both chauffeur, footman and butler, came in to ask her to attend Mr Loamer in the library, she followed him, resolved to have her own way in the matter which was to be the subject of their interview.

To her surprise, George Loamer was alone. There was a greater cause for apprehension in his face. It was deathly pale, and on a corner of the desk where he sat was a half-emptied decanter. That he had employed this to some purpose she gathered from his indistinct speech. This was the most astonishing thing of all, for she knew him as an abstemious man, who limited himself to a glass of claret with his dinner; indeed, she never remembered before seeing whisky in the house.

'Close both doors, Milton,' he said, unsteadily, and he waited until the outer door was closed before he spoke. 'Sit down, October.'

There was on his desk a mass of papers. To one of these she saw a number of seals affixed.

He licked his dry lips – and his lips were often dry in these days.

'October,' he began, 'I've been thinking all day how I should talk to you, what I should say to you, and I have decided to tell you the truth.'

For a moment her heart nearly stopped beating. Why she should think so, she did not know, except that some dormant gift of instinct kindled to life, but she realised in a flash that she was speaking with a ruined man.

He saw her change of face and read in her eyes something of her dismay.

'I haven't stolen your money,' he said loudly. 'Your fortune is practically intact ... I couldn't touch it. God knows if I could, I should have used it.'

She could only look at him open-mouthed.

'I'm going to tell you the truth.' His face was drawn and old-looking. 'I'm as near to ruin as I can be. Your money would stave it off ... save me perhaps something ... terrible.'

'Ruin?' she said incredulously. 'Why, I thought – '

'I've been speculating for years. Somebody ... somebody I'm rather fond of is very extravagant – terribly extravagant. She thinks no more of a thousand pounds than you or I think of a penny. She just throws it away with both hands ... mad schemes ... thousands – nearly a million gone, and I've got to get right, October. I'm putting myself at your mercy. I had all sorts of lies to tell you, but now I'm telling you the truth. I want you to marry me. I've arranged everything.'

She shook her head.

'That is impossible,' she said quietly. 'I'm terribly sorry for you, Mr Loamer, but I can do nothing. Perhaps if I lent you a little – ?'

He shook his head.

'I must have the whole. Less than that is no use to me. If I had that I could stop the – the other thing. It is killing me, the worry of it. She doesn't mind. She's like a great general who does not trouble who dies so long as there is victory at the end.'

Who was the mysterious 'she'? October Jones guessed, but guessed wrong.

He was talking now rapidly, disjointedly, and it was difficult to follow from his slurred speech the mind behind it. He picked up a telegraph form and waved it. At any other moment his gesture would have been ridiculous, but she felt the tragedy that lay beyond the gesture.

' ... this is a respite ... nothing happened. They missed him ... I could wire them and stop everything if you'd help me. You shall be as free as the air, October. I won't ask anything of you but the money.'

From time to time his eyes went over to the big French clock above the mantelpiece. He was like a man who was compressing into too limited a time a task beyond his power …

'I had all sorts of schemes, but none of them seemed as possible as this – telling you the truth, throwing myself on your mercy. Will you do this for me, October?'

Perspiration was rolling down his white face; he was like a man in mortal agony.

October shook her head.

'I couldn't do it, Mr Loamer, I couldn't, I couldn't,' she said in a low voice. 'I'm dreadfully sorry, but … '

He sank back in his chair, a huddled, wretched figure, and his white hand waved weakly towards the door.

'Sorry … sorry,' he mumbled. 'I hoped you would save … '

She did not hear the rest of the sentence distinctly.

Her mind was in a whirl as she came back to the drawing-room. For five minutes she stood staring out into the dusk, her heart beating uncomfortably, trying to eradicate from the disorder of her mind the dull patch of fear that was widening every second …

Milton came in with a cup of coffee on a silver platter. He was his dark, inscrutable self. She took the cup with a trembling hand and was grateful for the refreshment, for her mouth was dry. Super-sensitive, too: the coffee had a queer, metallic taste to it.

Milton put down the tray and waited, though she nodded him to go. He waited because a half-hysterical Mr Loamer had instructed him to be near her when the drug took effect.

IV

Rain was happening rather than falling as the mud-covered racing car turned into the smelly drabness of Seven Sisters Road. There was just enough mist to surround every street lamp with a ghostly nimbus, just enough rain to keep the ground mist in movement.

The big machine roared up the glassy hill to Finsbury, skidding a little on the tramlines and more than a little when the brakes went on in obedience to the traffic policeman's signal. The driver, wet to the skin, stared gloomily ahead. His unshaven face was ludicrously mud-stained. The red-bearded man huddled up by his side scarcely opened his weary eyes. He had touched the deeps of physical discomfort: wet, chilled to the bone, every muscle in his body aching, he could sleep – if such a coma into which periodic flashes of reality penetrated could be called sleep.

The policeman waved them on, and with a splutter the car headed for the Holloway Road; came presently to the gloom of the Outer Circle about Regent's Park, turned through the gate that leads to Avenue Road, and stopped in the middle of the road before a small house that stood apart from its fellows. The passenger was nudged to wakefulness and, climbing down, the driver unlocked the door of a garage that was flush with the house and, sending the machine in a semi-circle, drove into the dark interior. The folding doors closed behind them.

'Put the light on,' said the passenger hoarsely. He had not spoken since they had left Royston.

His companion answered in a queer, quavering voice that was made up half of fear and half of sheer sickness.

'Where? Where's that switch? ... God, isn't it cold and horrible! Here it is.'

A light glowed overhead and the driver got down painfully, stretched his back with a grimace and groaned.

'I'm wetter than you if it comes to that ... *she's* probably dead! That's what I bin thinkin' all the ways from Bishop's Stortford. Suppose she's dead ... an' suppose we're held up by some fool policeman ... you know what these Essex coppers are ... s'pose they take a peek inside the boot, hey? An' suppose she's dead ... Mr Byrne!'

He wiped the back of his hand across his face and left a blacker smear. His age was something more than forty. A thin face, the valleys of flesh emphasized by high and prominent cheek-bones, and two small pale eyes set close together, were amongst his unattractions. It was rather difficult to recognise Milton the inscrutable. His companion, for all his fortitude, had the appearance of a drowned rat. He had stripped his thin, inadequate waterproof, his sleeves were clinging wetly to his bony wrists.

'Say, if she's dead, she's dead,' he said shortly, dived into his waisted pocket and produced a key.

In the streamlined back of the car was a square trap door which, raised, in ordinary cars forms a seat. Unlocking this, he pulled up the flap. But no seat came in to view. In the commodious well was the cramped and huddled figure of a girl. She lay as he had placed her. The doubled-up cushion that braced her back against the side of the machine had not moved.

Kneeling astride of the cavity, he stooped and drew up head and shoulders. The driver helped awkwardly, and stood watching fearfully as Red Beard examined the figure they had laid on the concrete floor of the garage.

October's face was colourless; there was no movement of breast or pulse. Red Beard let the cold hand fall. The driver, scanning his face anxiously, saw doubt written there.

'We ought to have bored a hole in the side – but there was air enough. Lift her up, Mr Byrne. Martha had best see her.'

Red Beard lifted the girl with scarcely an effort and, leading the way, the passenger passed through the back door of the garage along a narrow garden path, and presently his key slipped into a lock.

'Don't forget the step,' he warned. 'I'll put a light on as soon as I've shut the door. Martha!'

He called softly. Somewhere at the end of the passage a crack of yellow light appeared as a door opened cautiously.

'It's me,' said Milton, as he closed the door on Red Beard and his burden. 'We've got her.'

The room door opened wider. The woman he addressed stood aside and watched incuriously as the silent figure was laid on a red velvet sofa.

Martha was very stout – her pale-blue kimono made her appear even stouter than she was. Her hair was brushed back daringly from a high forehead – daringly because attention was invited to a big and shapeless face.

'I got through to Four Beeches to-night,' she said. Her voice was very deep and hoarse and yet monotonous. 'I told "O" to get the place ready. Is the governor going down?'

'Yes, yes,' said Milton testily. 'Just take a look at this girl. Is she dead?'

Martha bent over the girl.

'If she's passed over, it's written,' she said sombrely. She was a dabbler in spiritualism. 'I had a message to get into touch with a newcomer to-night. Maybe it's her.'

' "She",' snarled Milton. 'How many times have I told you not to say "her" when you mean "she"?'

Red Beard blinked from one to the other. He was a man of action and realised that this was not the moment for pedantry.

'Say, take a good look!' he said. 'Try her heart ... '

Martha fingered the bosom of the stained dress.

'She's alive,' she said. 'What did you give her?'

'The needle – the other side of Royston. She came round from the dope, so I gave her the needle.'

Milton ran his hand through his scanty hair with a grimace of pain. It was as if he had remembered something unpleasant.

Martha was still staring blankly at the girl on the sofa.

'She'd be called pretty, I suppose,' she asserted. 'Thin – I wish I was thin. She's got a fateful face. I'll bet she's psychic. Them kind of faces frequently is.'

Milton groaned.

' "Them"! Listen. Get my box. And have the little room ready. You'll have to sit up with her till morning. She goes on to Hampshire to-morrow night.'

Red Beard was drying his nose with a handkerchief.

'Maybe you can fix her so that she can start to-night,' he suggested. 'I got to get along.'

Milton and the woman looked at one another dubiously, and Red Beard went on:

'He said he'd have a proper car calling for her about one in the morning. That's in a few hours. He'd have sent her down that way from Newmarket, only he didn't want his car to be recognised.'

'What about the servants?' asked Martha. 'They'll talk.'

Milton's nerves were a little frayed.

'Servants!' he snarled. 'Are there any servants at Market

Chase? You know they come from the village every morning.'

Red Beard intervened again.

'I've got work to do. Gotta meet a guy who ought to come one way and is coming another, see?'

Milton did not see. Martha was busy with the unconscious girl.

'He ought to come Boo-loyne, but Lenny says he's doubled back to Havre.'

'What are you talking about?' he asked Milton impatiently.

Red Beard vouchsafed no explanation.

At one o'clock in the morning a policeman patrolling Avenue Road saw a big closed car draw up to a house which he knew had been let furnished a week or two before. It was not unusual to see cars, closed or otherwise, in this exclusive thoroughfare at such an hour. In view of the rain that pelted down, he would have been surprised if it had not been a closed car. He made the circuit of his beat, and came back to find that the machine had disappeared. It was well on its way to Hampshire, with a girl who was still half-conscious and wholly miserable. She did not know that the arm that supported her was the arm of an expert gunman, or that the broad shoulder that supported her head was the shoulder of Red Beard. If she had known, she would not have cared.

She woke dizzily on a morning, to find herself in a small attic room, poorly furnished. The one high window that admitted light was heavily barred, and when she dragged herself on shaking limbs to the door, she discovered it was locked.

For an hour October Jones lay motionless, catching wildly at the threads of reality. And then Martha came in with a tray. She knew Martha, with her oily face and her pince-nez, and did not greet her. The woman put the tray on a small table and drew it to the side of the bed.

'Here's your breakfast, Mrs Loamer,' she said shrilly.

The girl sat up quickly, her head reeling.

'Mrs Loamer?' she repeated in a cracked voice.

Martha nodded, evidently with satisfaction.

'You've been two days down here,' she said. 'You were married to Mr Loamer last night by special licence. I'm surprised you don't remember.'

She went out quickly, closed and locked the door behind her, and left October Jones to grapple with her grotesque problem.

First of all she had drunk a cup of coffee at Market Chase. Then she was lying very uncomfortably in a sort of box, and something sharp pricked her forearm ... then she was in a car. These were the fragments from which she must rehabilitate the lost hours. The tea revived her. She nibbled at a piece of toast, but could not eat.

And then she saw on the tray a folded envelope, the cover unfastened. She pulled out the paper inside and read the long slip uncomprehendingly. It was a marriage certificate, as far as she knew what marriage certificates were. A marriage performed between ... There was her name, and 'George Augustus Loamer, bachelor, of independent means.' And a flourishing signature at the bottom.

It wasn't possible – it couldn't be. She was dreaming. Presently she would wake up at Market Chase ...

The key turned in the lock. It was Martha, and Martha evidently primed to supply such information as was requested.

The girl's head ached no longer; she was still a little dizzy, and although her heart thumped with unpleasant distinctness, she had regained something of her normal calm.

'I've brought you a paper.' Martha's thumb dug into an announcement on the front page of the sheet she laid on the bed. 'There's the announcement.'

October took up the journal mechanically. 'Loamer – Jones. By special licence ... ' She put the paper back on the bed and asked no questions. The stout Martha was obviously disappointed.

'It happened in this very house – ' she began.

'Thank you, I don't want to know anything about it,' said October. 'Am I to be kept in this room?'

Martha hesitated.

'You can come downstairs if you like, but you'll have to stay with me all the time. Mr Loamer isn't coming back till this afternoon.'

'Where is this place?'

Again Martha seemed reluctant to speak. 'Somewhere in the country,' she said vaguely.

And then an inspiration came to the girl.

'Is this Four Beeches?' She knew of Mr Loamer's Hampshire farm, and had once expressed a desire to accompany him on one of his infrequent visits.

'Yes, this is Four Beeches. You can see the trees from your window. But don't you try to wander round, Miss Jones.'

'It was Mrs Loamer a little time ago,' said the girl coldly.

'I mean Mrs Loamer,' said Martha, in perturbation. 'There's bogs all round. One of my cows got drowned there last week. This is the wildest part of Hampshire; we're only a few miles from Salisbury Plain. If you want to go downstairs I'll come back for you in a few minutes.'

October nodded, and when the door was locked upon her, climbed to a chair and looked out of the barred windows. The prospect was bleak and comfortless; rain was still falling, but it was warmer. She looked across a stark stretch of uncultivated land to a ridge of wood-covered hills. There was no sign of road, or any other human habitation.

She poured water from a ewer into a shallow basin and bathed her face: and the cold of the water revived her. It was an altogether different October Jones (or was it Loamer?) who went down the narrow stairway to a paved hall and was ushered by her custodian into a stuffy little sitting-room.

If she had any doubts as to her liberty of movement, those doubts were soon removed. Martha left her alone in the room but she locked the door on her, and despite the closeness of the day the windows were fastened and apparently immovable.

October Jones had brought the newspaper with her and now read the notice through word by word. It was not possible. The whole thing was a fantastic invention. What minister would marry an unconscious girl? She tossed the paper aside, and presently, in utter boredom, retrieved it and skimmed the news.

It was then that she read the little paragraph about the tramp who had broken into a Southampton store and stolen a pistol. By a trick of mind, this was the one item in the newspaper which remained with her, though why she should be interested in the picturesque thefts of tramps she could not divine.

At midday Martha served her lunch, and graciously permitted her the run of the house. She saw no other servants, but she heard a man's voice speaking through a closed door, and she thought she recognised Milton, and this recognition was justified a little later, when she caught a glimpse through the window of a man's back as he passed rapidly across the stable yard and disappeared behind the heavy door of a barn.

It was four o'clock that afternoon when George Loamer arrived, and there was nothing of the Mr Loamer she had seen at Newmarket. His step was jaunty, his manner bright, affable, self-assured. Whatever was the stimulant which produced this new return to his old confidence, it was effective.

He came into the little sitting-room as he might have stepped into his own office, silk-hatted, frock-coated, an incongruous figure in such rural surroundings.

'Ah, my dear October!' He greeted her with the warmth of a best friend. 'So you are yourself again! Well, well, that is splendid – and how wonderful of you to agree at the last moment. You have saved me from a very embarrassing situation.'

He was expecting an outburst, she guessed, and was disconcerted by her silence.

'As I said before,' he went on, and this time it needed an effort to maintain his manner of assurance. 'the marriage is a mere matter of convenience. Possibly in a year or so you would like a – um – divorce.' In spite of himself he winced at the word, for Mr George Loamer was a highly respectable man.

'Will you tell me just what the position is, Mr Loamer?' she asked. 'Of course I'm not married to you: that stupid certificate wouldn't deceive a child. You can buy the blanks for a penny each at any law stationer's.'

He was taken aback at this, winked at her quickly, as a man might wink who was suddenly confronted with a light of devastating brightness.

'Eh? Law stationer's? Come, come, October.' He made an heroic effort to recover his lost ground.

'You brought me here – why? Of course you drugged me: my head was horrible this morning. And you know better what are the consequences than I. I think they are rather serious, aren't they? If you will take me back to London now, I am prepared to say no more about the matter.'

'You were married to me – ' he began shrilly.

She shook her head with a little smile.

'It is a little childish, isn't it? I don't know in what bright mind this stupid plan was conceived, or who was the tragic fool – '

His face went suddenly red.

'You will be careful how you speak, October,' he said sharply. 'I will not allow you to insult ... '

He stopped suddenly and went off at a tangent.

'You're married, and that's the end of it. You will stay here for a few days, before we go to the Continent together. Our marriage was announced in the daily press.'

She could have laughed in any other circumstances. It was inconceivable that a man of his age and experience could be so desperately foolish. And yet there was something more than folly in the situation, she realised; a danger more sinister than she would admit to herself.

The interview was not prolonged. She excused herself and went back to her room, to be summoned to dinner a few hours later. In that time she had made a reconnaissance of the room. The lock was a cheap one, and, had she the strength, she could have broken it. It was while she was making an examination that she remembered something that the village carpenter who had been called in to repair a door at Market Chase had said.

'In an ordinary house, miss, one door key will open any lock – they're all made alike.'

She wondered if this was so and, going down to dinner in the long and dismal dining-room lit by oil lamps, she made a furtive and successful effort to extract the key from the door of that room and slip it onto the bosom of her dress.

Again Mr Loamer's mood had changed. He was taciturn and gloomy throughout the meal, drank incessantly. Not one word did he say about her affairs, and she was relieved. The only remark that he made concerned the good terms upon which he stood with the neighbouring farmers. There had been a number of tramp robberies in the district, and the police efforts to trace and capture the thieves had been ineffectual. There was some suggestion of the farmers taking the matter into their own hands. Mr Loamer repeated this fact several times, and she wondered if there was any peculiar importance in such a decision.

Martha took her back to her room, and it was then that she discovered she was not the only inmate of the house. Again she saw the figure of Milton vanishing down the long corridor. He carried a food-laden tray in his hands.

'That's a man we're got in for the day,' said Martha hurriedly, and her very anxiety to convey this information emphasised the identity of the chauffeur.

She sat down on her bed to wait. The evening had grown close and the room was almost airless. Looking up, she saw a long coat hanging behind the door. It had not been there that morning. It was her own, and by the feel and appearance of it she guessed that it had been rough-dried. She took this down. If it was raining, it might be useful.

She waited till the house was in silence, and then, recovering the key, she tried it in the door, and to her joy it turned. She fastened the lock again with a wildly beating heart, and waited for the hours to pass. Mr Loamer's unsteady feet sounded on the stairs. They passed her door, and she heard him muttering something to himself. Then somebody called him softly, and there was a whispered colloquy in the passage. She heard his exclamation of anger, and –

'Here, in the neighbourhood? He can't have got ... '

She did not hear the rest, but after a while:

'You can trust me and Lenny – yes, sir!'

Red Beard! So he was here! Why had Loamer to trust him and Lenny, the little fat Italian?

The hands of the small alarm clock on the washstand pointed to eleven when, with trembling fingers, she inserted the key in the lock. For an hour no sound had broken the silence; the house was quiet. The key turned with more quietness than she had expected, and in another second, with her coat over her arm, she was tiptoeing down the stairs. She crossed the lobby and felt for the fastenings of the great front door. It was not only bolted and chained, but locked, the key had been removed, and she had left her own key upstairs. There must be another way out. Holding her breath, she crept down the long passage – it seemed of interminable length. Presently she felt an angle of wall. Here the passage turned. She had taken two steps when –

A door opened in front of her somewhere, and the opposite wall was illuminated with a square of faint light. She drew back into the long passage, her heart racing.

'Why don't you take him by train?'

It was Milton talking in a low voice.

'Take him by train?' growled the second man. 'Where's your sense?'

'What about a car?' suggested Milton.

'Put him in a car and he squeals like hell. I can take the road for it. It will be a bit of a job to get round London, but we can sleep up at night. I don't know why he shifted him at all.'

Milton whispered something. There was a surly good-night. A door opened and another closed. October waited another five minutes before she moved. Looking round a corner, she saw that one of the doors was ajar. There was a pencil of light showing, and a murmur of voices came to her ears. Faint as it was, it showed her a way of escape. At the end of the passage a door was wide open. Evidently a fire was burning there, for she saw the spasmodic leap of flames, caught a glimpse of a large table. That was the kitchen, and a way out.

She took off her shoes and went softly along the passage. As she came abreast of the door that was ajar, she saw to her horror that it had swung open a little wider. She had a glimpse of the broad back and bullet head of a tall man, and beyond him, lying on a little truckle bed, staring up fearfully, a little bald, old gentleman, who was making queer whimpering sounds.

'Shut up!' growled the big man. 'If you don't shut up I'll beat your head off!'

Setting her teeth, she darted into the kitchen. There was no light but the fire. She saw the yawning opening of the scullery, and guessed that the way out lay there. Later that night she was to explore yet another scullery, but in her wildest imaginings she could not have foreseen this.

The key was in the lock; she turned it, drew back the bolts noiselessly and stepped out into the open air and, stopping only to slip on her shoes, ran across the badly paved courtyard. Her foot was on a low fence when something rose up in front of her.

'Don't move or I'll shoot!' whispered a voice fiercely, and at that moment there was a flicker of lightning and she gazed into a face hideous beyond her worst dreams.

V

'Oh, a woman!' he said. 'What the dickens are you – '

'Help me get away, help me get away, for God's sake!' She was frantic with terror.

In another instant he had gripped her arms and lifted her to the ground.

'What's the trouble?'

She did not answer. Her teeth were chattering with fear. With his hand on her arm, he guided her to behind the barn, into a little ruined cowshed.

'Come in here; you'll be all right.'

He drew her in, stirred the little fire that smouldered into a blaze.

A tramp! Her heart sank at the sight. He was less savoury than most tramps, and more dangerous, for he was carrying a serviceable automatic pistol. He was not pleasant even as tramps go. His face was blotched and swollen; he carried a week's growth of beard; one eye was recovering from the violent impact of a fist, delivered a week before by a brother tramp whom he had awakened at an inconvenient moment. His collar and shirt were grimy; his apology for a jacket had bottomless pits for pockets; on the back of his head he maintained an ancient derby hat, badly dented, the rim rather lacking. He saw her amazement and grinned, but his amusement was short-lived. Somewhere nearby he heard a voice call gruffly: 'What's that light, Lenny?' In an instant he had stamped on the flames, half-lifted, half-dragged her through the crumbling doorway of the hut. She thought he was drunk; there was a faint aroma of spirits in the air.

'I want you to take me to London,' she whispered urgently. 'Please, please!'

'Why not go to the police?' he answered, intelligently enough.

She shook her head. What had she to complain of? Her life had not been threatened. This horrible marriage ... it might be true after all.

'Can you help me to get ... somewhere, away from this horrible place?'

She heard him chuckle.

'Sure,' he said, and added, unnecessarily: 'My name's Robin.'

There was no sound of pursuit. Robin was walking ahead of her – she saw the nearly white sleeve of his tattered shirt and, quickening her pace, overtook him.

'Where's that?'

He was pointing, she guessed.

'I don't know the place.'

He rubbed his forehead.

'Looks like a road – there must be another way – a path over the fields.'

She considered.

'Isn't there a village somewhere near – we might find help there – '

'Not the help I want,' said the tramp quickly. 'I want to be a wicked human. Maybe you're keen on getting into the angel class.'

He stood uncertainly. Ahead was the gate and the road. Behind she heard somebody roar her name.

'This way.'

She caught him by the sleeveless coat and dragged him between bushes along a track scarcely visible in daylight. The path brought them to grass and trees and an occasional view between the apple trees of a far-away yellow light. Presently they were clear of the orchard and traversing a rough stretch of field where Martha grazed her cows. There was a big barn here, its bulk showing blackly against the sky. Beyond was rough going, a pool where the cows drank and sheer waste land where nothing grazed or grew.

'There is a storm somewhere,' said Robin. October had seen the lightning. 'Following the river valley.'

She stopped suddenly.

'What are you – what nationality? You're not English?'

'American.' His voice sounded a little impatient.

She drew a long breath.

'Oh ... I'm British.'

'You surprise me.'

She could not see his face; she had to suppose his sarcasm from tone and attitude. Her lips were tight pressed.

'I'm English – nothing will ever make me anything but English.'

'Oh ... ' He was inclined to be rude, she thought. 'You said you were British just now – I hate people who can't make up their minds. Where are we going?'

'Where *are* we going? Where do you want to go?'

'London – and we've got to get there on foot. Where does this bring us – right here, I mean?'

She told him there was a road ahead of them. Though she had never been to Four Beeches, she knew the farm and the country about.

'Is there a little wood – road goes through it?' he asked eagerly. And, surprised, she said that there was. They had reached the fence which marked the boundary of the farm when he hissed:

'Don't speak – kneel!'

She obeyed and heard somebody talking, and after a while saw the flare of a match.

'Flat down ... in this dip!' He set her an example and

sprawled face downward on the moist grass. She fell beside him, her heart racing.

There was no cause for that wild excitement, she told herself, and yet she knew that there was an enormous, a vital reason. There was danger: a vague sense of peril lifted the hairs of her neck. She found herself glaring towards the road and hating the men who were walking in so leisurely a fashion towards them. Nearer and nearer. One stopped to strike another match. They were less than six yards from where the two were lying. She glimpsed a fat, broad face and had a flash of a red beard.

'You certainly put your name in lights, Lenny!' said Red Beard disparagingly. 'We ought to have come out with a band.'

'Huh!' grunted the other. 'What's that matter? He's not here ... not in miles.'

'I saw him, I tell you. The boss 'phoned me at Aldershot and I saw him crossing the heath. If you'd been around I'd have got him.'

'Had to go up to the station ... that fly cop ... '

The voices grew indistinct; they became a murmur. Came a growl and rumble of thunder, and when it died away there was silence.

'Are they looking for you?' she whispered.

'Yes. They don't know that you have got away from Four Beeches.'

His voice was steady: he seemed suddenly a very capable tramp. As he rose, the western skies throbbed palely with lightning, and she saw the glint of something in his hand.

'Don't stub your toe against the fence,' he whispered. 'Wood sounds carry. Is there a gate?'

'Farther along ... '

'Down!'

He had seen the faint speck of a cigar end: the men were coming back. This time the hiding pair had an advantage. A small ridge of earth ran parallel with the fence; behind this they were safely screened.

The two strollers stopped opposite to them. Apparently one seated himself on the fence: they listened, heard the scrape of his shoes on the rail.

' ... back in the wood on the other side of town, I bet. Ought to have combed that wood, Lenny. If I hadn't been a bonehead, I'd a got him at Havre.'

A silence.

'He's got a gun,' said another voice.

'Like hell he has! That's newspaper lyin'. Fellers don't smash a store to get a gun ... well, maybe it wasn't a store, but I reckon the bookkeeper's office at a plant is as good as a bank.'

'Newspaper said – '

'Newspaper!' He added an appeal to his Deity.

Another long silence. The scent of a good cigar was wafted towards and over the hillock. The sound of their footsteps receded. Raising his head, Robin took an observation.

'I'm a store robber,' he murmured. 'That's certainly good!'

Ten minutes passed before he got up and helped her to rise.

'Where is the gate?'

She walked a little ahead of him: he must have seen the coat she carried was trailing; he took it from her without a word.

The gate was found and was half open. They went through the road, which was uneven but infinitely easier to walk upon than the field. The grass had been heavy with dew – she felt the front of her dress was soaked.

'There's a house up in these woods; haunted. You're not afraid?'

'The Shepherd's house,' she said, remembering.

'That's it. Hanged himself, didn't he? Tramps never go there ... rather sleep in the rain. They think it is unlucky. Terribly superstitious people, tramps. Am I walking too fast?'

'No.' A hundred yards farther on: 'You're not drunk now.'

He turned his head sideways to her.

'I never was drunk. I'm just all in. I keep thinking you're – someone else. And my legs are all crazy. I didn't sleep last night. I jumped a ride on a freight train, a goods train from Southampton night before that, but one of the train hands found me and booted me off. I could sleep standing to-night. But I'm dizzy all right – '

The road began to ascend. She had so often walked this way that she could have gone forward blindfolded. Larches appeared on either hand and the road became a track. Now they were in great darkness; the far-off lightning was helpful, the sky reflection came down to them through the tree tops.

'It is to the left somewhere ... there are two steps up the bank.'

They walked more slowly now, searching for the path to the Shepherd's house. A flicker of light in the sky, and they saw the steps – two rough-hewn slabs of sandstone, worn by the feet of the suicide. She went first, paused at the top and pointed – at least he thought she was pointing. The storm was coming nearer; the heaven lit up in a quivering succession of flashes. He saw a low-roofed shack, a shutter that hung by one hinge, a pitiful little portico drooping on one pillar.

'Home!' said Robin magnificently.

The door was fast, but a window gave him entrance. After a while she heard his footfall in the passage and the squeaking of a latch. It took a perceptible time to open the door, and then it only yielded far enough to admit her.

'Hinges gone,' he said briefly.

He pushed the door tight and then, striking a match, lit a piece of candle which he took from a pocket on the inside of his coat. The passage was inches deep in debris. Dead leaves had found their way here, and scraps of discoloured rags showed under the accumulations of dust. Across the passage ran a beam of unpainted wood, and screwed into the wood was a large hook. She saw this and ... the forgotten shepherd, whose sole memorial this tumbledown house was, had hanged himself.

'Ugh!'

He looked at her gravely.

'Not scared?' His eyes went up to the hook. '*That* wasn't it. Used to hang bacon there. He *did* it in the wood – on a tree somewhere. So they say. Lost his wife and went mad – before you were born. So they say.'

'So who say?' a little impatiently.

He jerked his head vaguely towards the moor; in reality he was indicating a scattered community.

'Tramps swop these yarns. I didn't understand them all –

they have a language of their own. Hold the light, will you, please?'

October took the candle from his hand and he lurched into a room that opened from the passage. He returned very soon, carrying a dusty and ragged blanket.

'There's an iron bed – the spring mattress feels good to me. Rusty, I think ... but springy. We'd better chance a light.'

The bed was a very dismal looking affair, but, as he said, the spring bottom was intact. He shook out the blanket and folded it pillow fashion.

'Warmish,' he said sleepily, 'but you'd better put your coat over you.'

She sat on the bed. Looked at him. He might have been good looking once. The bristly face, the bruised eye, the puffy redness on one cheek ... October shook her head.

'What is the matter with your face?' she asked.

He was surprised by the question.

'Generally or particularly?' he asked, and touched his cheek. 'This? Wasps – it happened in France. I slept one night near a wasp nest – they woke me in the morning. Those old Inquisitors missed something. Go to sleep.'

She kicked off her shoes and lay down, pulling her coat over her. The mattress was largely soft, but it was made up of little steel links and her dress was thin ... she would be like a tattooed lady in the morning. He had seated himself in a corner of the room and blown out the candle. Presently she heard his deep breathing; once he snored.

Through the unshaded window she could see the sky lit red and blue at irregular intervals. The house shook and shivered with every crash of thunder. And then the rain came down. It rattled and drummed on the iron roof, beat against the broken window pane ...

'Seep ... peep ... peep!'

The roof was leaking somewhere; the drip and drop of water sounded close at hand. Between thunder rolls she heard the breathing of Robin ... she was dozing when he spoke in his sleep.

'Silly fool,' he muttered. 'Silly fool!'

Whether he was talking of himself or to somebody who belonged to the life that was veiled, or of her, she could only speculate upon.

She fell asleep dreamless ... she woke slowly with the consciousness that somebody was holding her hand ... a bristly cheek was near to hers. She opened her lips to scream and a firm hand closed her mouth.

VI

October was very wide awake now. She did not struggle, but gripped at the hand which covered her mouth, conserving all her strength to pry loose this suffocating pad of muscle and bone.

'Don't make a sound!' he was breathing. 'Terribly scared you'd shout ... somebody prowling outside the house.'

She nodded. The hand was drawn away, the bristly face was removed.

'Sorry!' he whispered. 'Can you get off the bed without raising a riot ... wait!'

His two hands went under her; she felt herself raised slowly.

'Creak – squeak!' went the rusty springs as they relaxed. He canted her gently, feet to floor, so that she stood with her back to the wall in which the window was set.

'Don't move!'

The storm had passed; she thought she detected the ghostly light of dawn in the room. Silence ... and then, outside, the cracking of a twig.

Robin the tramp crouched under the window. She could only see a splodge of something a little blacker than the blackness of the room.

The window darkened; hands were fumbling with the latch. She heard the low murmur of a querulous voice. Suddenly a brilliant circle of light appeared on the opposite wall: the man outside was searching the room with an electric lamp. The circle moved left and right, up and down; focussed on the end of the rusty bed and paused there undecidedly. She saw Robin clearly now, huddled under the window; he was gripping a steel rod that, attached to the window, had once regulated its opening. She wondered why the man outside had failed to find a way in. The light went.

'Get to the door ... along the passage to the right ... take your shoes but don't put them on!'

She nodded agreement to the sibilant instructions, gathered her shoes and tiptoed along the passage until a door barred further progress. Here she waited. Presently she heard him coming towards her.

'Is it open?' he whispered, and went past her.

The passage was so narrow that she felt the brush of his shirt sleeve on her face. The door was unlocked but noisy. The enemy was at the front door by now, rattling the handle. Robin the tramp waited until the sound came again and then, putting his shoulder to the obstruction, pushed. With a grind and a jar it opened. Reaching back, he caught her by the arm and pulled her through. They were in a kitchen which smelt of earth and damp. A second door was here ... he felt for it, groping along wet walls. Overhead the roof had partly vanished.

A thudding sound shook the little house ... another. Robin tugged at the door and it opened with a groan; the scent of wet leaves and balsam came to October's grateful nostrils.

'Got your coat?' His lips were close to her ear. She did not mind the bristly cheek now. 'Good! Follow me – you'll get your feet wet but that won't kill you. Hold my sleeve ... when I stoop, do the same.'

He stepped out into the tangle of what had once been a garden. Noiselessly he moved towards the encircling wood, she creeping behind him. Her stockings were soaked; once she trod on a thorn and needed all her self-control to repress a cry – as it was, she made some sort of sound, for he half turned. They were circling towards the town road; if it had been light they could not have seen the Shepherd's shack when he stopped.

'Put on your shoes – I expect your feet are wet.'

She held on to his arm with one hand and pulled on her shoes one by one with the other. Her feet were sodden and the soles of her silk stockings in rags. But she was glad to have leather between foot and earth.

'No hurry: they will take some time exploring the hut,' he said, still whispering. 'And the trees will spoil Lenny's style – he likes the great open spaces where men are men!'

Something amused him: she heard him laughing in staccato gasps. He was moving more swiftly, and the distance between them and the shack must have been considerable when they struck a path that ran downhill, the trees began to thin, and then he caught tight hold of her arm and stopped.

She saw the figure, too.

It was smoking a cigarette. There was just enough light in the sky to reveal an indistinct outline. A man, and he was sitting on a fallen tree to their left front.

Behind them, somebody shouted; it sounded faint and comfortably far. The man on the tree trunk got up and strolled slowly up the path, but unexpectedly deviated to his right. He passed the watching pair not a dozen yards away – evidently he had missed the path.

'Hullo!' he called.

'They've been here – but they've gone.' Still faintly.

It was Red Beard's voice; she recognised its deep raucousness.

The smoker passed out of sight ... still stooping. Robin went on ... stopped again and pointed.

In the fold of the little hill she saw three gleaming lights, two white, one red.

'A car,' he breathed.

By the position of the lights she saw that the bonnet of the machine was turned towards Ash.

Stealthily he crept towards the lights and, holding fast to his sleeve, she followed. One swift look round.

'Jump in!' he said, and she scrambled aboard.

She did not realise that the engines were running until he was by her side. He gripped the gear lever, looked back again. They were moving with little or no sound. The springs of the machine took the strain of the uneven surface, nearer and nearer to the white road they stole. Then she heard a shout behind, but, looking round, could see nothing against the dark background of hill and wood.

The car was going faster. Something buzzed past her cheek; she thought it was a nocturnal beetle and instinctively put up her hand to brush her face.

Robin the tramp slowed to take the turn; and now Ashleigh was behind them and the car was flying towards Farnham. She sat huddled in a corner of the seat, watching and yet not watching the country fly past. Barn and farm-house, rail crossing, stretch of rolling country, now a steep hill, tree-furred, now a dead town with an ugly iron church and none to watch their passage but a cat.

Once they passed a lake and saw at the end of it a miniature Niagara. It was growing lighter. They passed a farm wagon.

Robin came to a fork and branched right, though it was clear that this was the poorer road. And so it proved. They bumped and swayed up a steep and slippery grade. The road became unrelieved rock, and when they had got beyond a great scar in the hillside, from which at some period stone had been quarried, the road ceased to be. Nevertheless, they continued, dodging between trees, avoiding, miraculously, a confusion of boulders that seemed to have been dropped for the especial purpose of checking their adventure. Coming over a razor-back ridge, he jammed on the brakes, and only in time, for from the crest the ground dropped steeply to the well-defined edge of a chasm.

'That's that,' said the tramp, and hoisted himself from his seat.

Before she could descend, he had put his hands about her waist and lifted her free of the machine. He walked to the top of the slope and looked back. The car tracks were visible on the grass if the search came so far. But beyond was the stone causeway (as he called it) and the lower slopes of the road had marks of wagon wheels in which his own might merge.

He strolled to the car, pulled from the back seat a folded rug and then 'whooped' softly. There was a basket here and a hold-all. He lugged them out, one after the other. Opening the lid, he looked in and grinned demoniacally (as October thought); then he unrolled the canvas carry-all.

'Here is a towel and soap – I can hear water up there,' he jerked his head to the higher slopes. ' 'Ware wire!'

She looked enquiringly at him.

' 'Ware – ?'

'Watch your step,' he translated.

She found the water; it was beautifully cold. When she came back to him with a light step, as rosy as the dawn that had broken, he took towel and soap from her and went up the hill. There was a ludicrous plaid patch on the back of his pants that seemed in keeping. She had seen the genus at such a distance as the stalls are from the stage. October watched him, chin in hand, until he disappeared behind the tangle of flowering hawthorns and laurel that hid the spring.

Out of the mad confusion of the night this fact emerged. The life of Mary October Jones, heiress at law, had in the twinkling of an eye become identified with that of 'Robin' – an unknown and most disreputable tramp.

And the situation did not seem unreal. She was part of his life. Red Beard was her deadly foe. She had thrilled and grown tense at a common danger. October never analysed her own emotions. She could pick to threads motives and causes, could reduce to formulae human eccentricities, but she never felt the urge to disintegrate her own soul that she might furnish sections for a microscope, or tested with the acid of other people's experience her own reactions. The man attached to the plaid patch was a fact. He could differ only from any other man in respect to his behaviour. So far he was entirely satisfactory. He had given her the spring bed (she *was* a tattooed lady, she had discovered after a limited investigation); he had told her to put on her shoes at exactly the right moment. She in his place would have done the same. He drove a car rather efficiently. He had probably stolen cars before. The plaid patch was not absurd, nor the sleeveless jacket. Probably his pants were hitched up with string and she had overlooked the old soup can that all tramps carry.

He came back very clean looking and surprisingly wholesome: when he opened the basket and offered her a sandwich she saw that his nails were immaculate. But he was a little shaky; his eyes bloodshot. They were grey eyes set well apart, but they were decidedly bloodshot. There was a vacuum bottle in the basket. The coffee steamed as he poured it into one of the cups that he had found in this heaven-sent canteen.

'Now,' he said, and sat down cross-legged, 'let's get everything right! I know you are here, I know that you were in the Shepherd's house – by the way, he *did* hang himself from that hook, but I thought it best to lie – and I know that in some mysterious fashion you have got yourself attached to me. But exactly why and how?'

She sat very upright at this. Was he joking? Apparently not. He was sipping at his cup, one reddish eye regarding her over its edge.

'You're taking me to London,' she said. 'I was married last night.'

He choked ... coughed, and put down the cup.

'I beg your pardon?'

'I was married to somebody two days ago,' she said. She did not think it necessary to name her husband.

By the rising horror that made his face more unpleasant, she gathered that he was shocked to the core.

'I told you so.'

'You're not serious?'

She nodded.

'I'm very serious. You don't remember?'

No, he did not remember. He was terribly bewildered.

She told him undramatically. And as she went on, he punctuated the story with startled 'Good lord's!'

'But you're really serious? You married – er – and you've run away?'

She was very serious, she said.

Robin covered his face with his hands and moaned.

'What a perfectly horrible nightmare!'

She was interested but not offended.

'Is it, Mr Robin – '

'Mr who?' he demanded, his eyes wide open.

'That is the name you gave – Mr Robin. I suppose you

dreamt that?'

He shook his head dispiritedly.

'No – that's my name all right – at least, it is my Christian-given name,' he said. 'What a perfectly ghastly thing to happen! I've no recollection – I suppose it was the fever. I'll tell you the truth. I had a bout of malaria and stole a bottle of Brother Loamer's whisky. Was I very – ?'

'You were – rather,' she said, 'in fact, very. You said you were sorry – '

'I was sober then,' grimly. 'What is or was your name?'

'Mary October Jones.'

'What a horrible name!' he groaned. 'Moses – *what* a name!'

She stiffened at this.

'I don't see anything "horrible" about it,' she said coldly. 'It is certainly unusual.'

'Unusual! What am I to call you?'

'You may call me October,' she replied.

'I'll be – I won't, anyway. What a swine!'

'Of course, if you regret the help you are giving me … ' she began stiffly.

His solemn eyes were fixed on hers.

'Don't let us start our disgraceful adventure with a quarrel,' he said sombrely. 'Have another sandwich.'

She took the sandwich because she was hungry.

'We will pack all the grub that is left,' he suggested. 'I don't think we shall be getting any eats as sumptuous as these for a very long time.'

He looked up at the sky.

'Seven o'clock – between that and eight. We ought to double back towards Ashleigh, then strike north-east. There is plenty of timber in this country, thank heaven! With luck we should find a place where we can sleep before nightfall.'

'Why does that red-bearded man want you? Have you committed a crime?'

He smiled with his eyes.

'Have I committed a crime? Yes. I burgled a factory; "plant" he called it, and pinched a gun. This is my chief offence. I don't mind *him*. It is the little fellow, the knife-throwing gentleman, who rattles me. He is rather wonderful – a South American, I suppose. Leonardo Dellamontez. And run! That fellow can sprint like a hare. You wouldn't think so to see him. Very fat and short in the leg. I shouldn't think he could sit a horse. But a real artist.'

He spoke dispassionately, if anything admiringly, of the knife-thrower. October had the illusion that they were sitting together on the grandstand watching Leonardo competing in some murderous Olympic game.

'You're not a real tramp, are you?' she asked.

'Sure as you're born!' he answered. 'Is that the right thing to say? Yes, I'm a tramp, but the County of Hampshire is not an ideal tramping ground. There is no merit in the exercise you get from strolling through a picture gallery. Now the Gobi Desert is real tramping! And the woolly lands beyond Urzra. That's tramping, too!'

She had a dim idea that the Gobi Desert was in China, but Urzra she could not place.

'Mongolia – it's Red now. Queer little place, full of Buddhist priests and dogs that will pull you down in the street and leave nothing but your watch and buttons.'

'But,' she insisted, 'you're tramping for ... for fun, for pleasure. It is a sort of holiday, isn't it? You aren't tramping because you've no money and ... well, because you can't get work?'

'I've got two shillings,' he said. 'Just now I'm tramping to save my life!'

'Why?'

He shook his head.

'I'd hate to tell you,' he said. 'If I did, you'd say what I say – Such Things Cannot Be!'

'But what *are* those things?'

He rose, gathered her cup and corked the vacuum bottle.

'Mediaeval things – things you hear about in the Valley of the Rhone and on the Rhine. The history of France is full of it, and England. That is what I am finding in this Europe of yours – just mad, impossible things that cannot be. You're another of 'em! Good lord!'

He was shaking his head at her.

'I really must have been tight!'

'Intoxicated,' she said. 'You're almost offensive.'

'Am I?' He was immediately penitent. His unsightly face drooped. 'Of course I am ... but I just feel that I *can* be offensive to you.'

She knew what he meant and was fairly well pleased.

VII

The way they took was a painful one. They traversed mile upon mile of sloping hill; she seemed, most of the time, to be walking alternately on the right side of her right foot and the left of the other. Both legs ached in turn, whilst the other went cramped. And yet she carried nothing. It was Robin who was loaded up with food and blanket. She did not even carry her own coat.

There was very little conversation. He admitted that he did not know the country at all; she was almost as ignorant. She had paid a visit to Hampshire – had spent a holiday within sight of Four Beeches – but she did not even know the names of relative positions of the towns. Twice she had been to Bournemouth, but the window of an express is a poor place to study topography. She knew Winchester, because she had taken motor trips from Bournemouth.

The position was intriguing, bizarre. She could hardly keep her eyes from the plaid patch. Once upon a time she had made a study of the Scottish tartans. It wasn't Stewart – Stewart is red; and it was not Cameron – that had a yellowish line in it (or was that Gordon?).

'Campbell!' she cried triumphantly.

'Eh?' He came round in alarm.

'That patch – on your trousers. It is a Campbell tartan!'

'Is it?' He screwed his head to see. 'I am not fearfully keen on the Campbells. So it is – how clever of you!'

As he lifted his jacket to examine the patch she saw the butt of a gun in his pocket. She had supposed the revolver, but had forgotten all about it.

'Isn't it very dangerous carrying a pistol in England?' she asked. 'I mean ... in your position?'

'Much more dangerous not to – especially now.'

He resumed his march and was talking over his shoulder, and then, at a tangent:

'I suppose you wouldn't have the slightest difficulty in getting a divorce?'

'I don't wish a divorce – yet,' she said calmly, and she heard him groan again. 'You're very ungallant,' she said.

'I am, aren't I? Very sorry. What is the best remedy for wasp stings?'

'Does it hurt?' She was sympathetic.

'A wee bit – nothing to make a fuss about. It rather irritates when one is hot. Hullo!'

He stood stock still. Ahead of them they heard the clop-clop of a woodman's axe, and as they stood, the swish and thud of falling timber.

They were walking along the wet floor of a little ravine. There was cover enough in case of necessity, thickly-growing clumps of dark laurel and fern-like laburnum. The walls of the little valley rose steeply. Looking up, he saw with some concern a small hut perched on the edge. But there was no sign of a man or his inevitable dog.

'Let's try this other face,' he suggested. 'I'm afraid that the unsparing woodmen are on the other side of that bluff.'

He went first and their progress was painfully slow. In half an hour he drew himself cautiously over the side of a rock. Before him was a beautiful sight, trees – pine, larch, birch – an impenetrable fairy woodland that belonged to dreams.

After a careful reconnaissance he signalled her to follow. They plunged into the cool twilight and silence. A game preserve of some kind, he thought; big, tame birds were strutting on the ground, a hen pheasant rose at his feet and went noisily to a less disturbed area. There were rabbits – he thought he saw a sleek black stoat.

The nest they found by accident – it was a saucer-like

depression in a small hillock, and was shielded from view, supposing anybody came, by low-growing bushes and high-growing ferns.

'We can't light a fire,' he said, as he spread the blanket for her to sit upon, 'but happily there is no need. You may find the ground damp. We will move on before night.'

'Where are we going?'

'Farnham,' he told her. 'Not exactly Farnham, but a few miles beyond. Hungry?'

He produced the vacuum bottle. The coffee was lukewarm but refreshing – what was left.

'But how do you know which way we're going?'

He felt in his hip pocket where the pistol was, and brought out a little compass. Because the nest was rather difficult to find, he broke off a small branch of a young tree and stuck it upright – more for her guidance than his.

'You don't mind being left alone? I want to do a little exploring.'

He was gone the greater part of two hours (she had become aware of her wrist-watch in the course of their morning march) and he returned, carrying three melons. There was a farm on the edge of the wood, he told her.

'Some swell lives there – it looks like one of those gentleman-farmers' places – pedigree cows and a good dancing floor. There was a wonderful pair of flannel trousers drying on a line, but I hadn't the nerve to raid 'em. Seen the newspapers?'

He took a sheet from his pocket. When he had lifted the melons he had also paid a visit to a gardener's shed. The newspaper had been lying on the bench.

'You're famous,' he said.

She unfolded the page, her mouth opened.

FIENDISH TRAMP STEALS THE BRIDE
OF LONDON FINANCIER.

COUNTY ROUSED. ARMED MEN SEARCHING
ALL NIGHT.

The account began.

> An amazing outrage has shocked Hampshire to its core. A famous London financier arrived at his farm, Four Beeches, Ashleigh, to spend his honeymoon with his young bride. About ten o'clock last night, the gentleman, returning to his library from a tour of the house, saw his wife struggling in the arms of a tramp. Before he could intervene he was felled by the intruder. When he recovered consciousness, his wife and the tramp had disappeared …

'Why … !' October's eyes were blazing. 'How *could* they! How could they! Oh!'

He was examining the news-sheet critically.

'That is a pretty good portrait of you. Most of these things flatter – I rather like your hair done that way.'

'I am going right back to Ashleigh to tell them they are liars!' she stormed. 'Liars! Oh, but it is too bad – '

'Worse to come – did you see the very latest? It is on the back page. You can't go back.'

With trembling hands she turned the newspaper and found the 'worse'.

> Has beautiful Mrs Loamer met with a terrible death at the hands of the mad tramp-fiend? That is the question all Hampshire is asking … '

'You see,' he explained gravely. 'You can't go back if you're dead: that would be an anticlimax and would be unpardonable. They would never forgive you. You had better stay dead for a week or two.'

' "Mad tramp" … ! I must do something!'

'Write to *The Times*,' he said soothingly.

'*The Times?* Don't be absurd. Can't you see what this means? Everybody will be searching for you – you'll never have a fair chance – they will shoot you like a dog if they come upon you here … or … or anywhere!'

'I suppose they would.' Only then such an idea occurred to

him, apparently. He was rather surprised. 'Pity one can't buy the afternoon extras – I'd like to know what Georgie says about the car. Do you bet?'

'I don't know what you mean,' she said bewildered.

'If you did, I would bet you that Georgie says nothing. Not a word – not a syllable. Of course, the farm hand may have seen us without being able to identify the machine I drove. In which case the search will shift nearer. Do you think you could sleep?'

She shook her head.

'Perhaps later – you're all nerved up by this infernal newspaper report. Sorry I brought it with me – I thought you would be amused.'

'Amused?' she scoffed.

As the afternoon wore on she began to feel drowsy and fell asleep for an hour. She woke to find him lying flat on his face at the edge of the 'saucer.' He had parted the ferns that obstructed his view, and as he looked back at her she guessed that her awakening owed nothing to chance.

'I saw a woman walking in the wood,' he said in a low voice. 'She was some distance away. Probably she belongs to the farm. I thought I had better kick you.'

'Did you kick me?' indignantly.

'We're tramps,' he said. 'The practice is very usual in our circle.'

Half an hour passed.

'I have been a brute,' he said, without turning his head. 'No, not over kicking you. That whisky of Loamer's was fierce. The man has no taste even in whisky. I'm still a little dithery, but I can think. When this woman has gone I will take you to the farm – at least to the outskirts. You'll find your way into the house and 'phone. I want you please to lie about me: say you left me on the Farnham road – wherever that may be.'

'Leave you?' She was aghast.

'Of course – you can't go around sleeping in woods … hunted and … God knows what. I'm being selfish really. It will be easier for me to get away. And you can tell them, of course, that you aren't dead and that I'm quite – as tramps go –

respectable. I was joking this morning about your not being able to go back because you were dead. But you English have no sense of American humour.'

She too was lying face downward now. Her hands was clasped under her chin.

'I'm late but I'm laughing,' she said calmly. 'How funny!'

'What?'

He screwed his head round to her and he was frowning. Much of the inflammation had left his face – one red weal ran from his ear and disappeared in the growth upon his chin.

'Do you really expect me to go to the farm and say "Please, I'm the stolen bride"? Have you any imagination?'

He scratched his nose, frowning deeper.

'I have – but I'd rather like to hear how yours is working.'

She flashed a quick smile. He had not seen her smile before, and the experience left him a little breathless.

'I'll tell you,' she nodded. 'I am met by the lady of the house – I relate my sad story. She looks at me ... oddly. Can't you see her eyebrows going up, can't you hear her saying "My poor child!" – supposing she is playing at farms and not a real slave-wife. And then she telephones to the police and maybe to Mr Loamer! And then she seeks her dearest friend, who maybe is staying with her and, closing the door so that the servants can't hear, tells *her*. And then they look at one another and one says "What do you think?" and the other says "Well – ", and then – '

'Oh, yes, yes!' Robin spoke hurriedly. He was actually embarrassed. 'Of course ... yes ... shut up!' This last outrageous piece of rudeness in a fierce whisper. 'The woman!'

October followed his example and, gently pressing back the ferns, looked.

The lady was very near to them. She strode manfully, using a black ebony walking cane. She was in black, and over her grey head she wore a Spanish mantilla. In point of inches she was enormous, and her thinness made her seem taller. Coming into a patch of sunlight, the swinging hands glittered dazzlingly. October saw this in spite of herself, for she was gazing awe-stricken at the face of the woman. Dead white, with dark-rimmed eyes and a nose that was grotesquely big and outstanding. Diamonds flashed at her ears, from her wrist, from the black corsage. She went on out of sight, and then October heard the man sigh.

'The managing director. Did you see her? Suffering snakes ... here!'

'Managing director – what do you mean?'

He shook his head; his staring eyes were still glued to the tree clumps around which she had disappeared. He was a comical picture of amazement.

'Well, I'll go sideways! The old sport!'

'Who is she?' October was a thought impatient.

'Mrs Loamer.'

The girl listened, stunned.

'Mrs Loamer!' she gasped. 'His – his – '

'Mother,' said Robin. 'The genius behind the colossal financier.'

She was dazed for a moment.

'But I never knew – she must be – '

'Seventy-six – I dined with her once: she has a swagger house in Kensington. She *is* staying at the farm. You can't go there.'

'I cannot because I will not,' said October correctly. 'I am going through to London. What will you do in London?'

'Nothing much.'

He was looking at her glumly; she felt that she had of a sudden become a worry to him.

'Anyway, I refuse to go back.' She very resolutely spoke her thoughts. He saw her shudder and was curious. Until that moment he had not considered very closely her relationship with Mr Loamer. He could both understand why she had married the sleek financier and why she had left him. He was rather too full of his own affairs to question her, even then.

A little while after this he pillowed his face on his arm and fell asleep. October took stock of the food. There were two very stale rolls, a small box of biscuits, three cakes of chocolate, and a segment of a pie, the latter carefully wrapped in thin white paper. They would not starve. There was, in addition to the vacuum bottle, a flat, military-looking water flask, which Robin had filled just before they climbed out of the ravine.

She sat patiently, her hands folded in her lap; it was her turn to keep guard. There was an importance in her vigil. Now and again she looked through the ferns, but saw nothing. The sun was sinking. Millions of tiny flies began to gyrate in great clouds under the spread of every tree. She heard more distinctly the 'tap tap tap' of a woodpecker.

'What time is it?' She did not know that he was awake.

'About seven – aren't you hungry?'

He sat up, rubbing his face vigorously.

'Starving,' he answered, and they supped together frugally. After they had wrapped up what food remained (and they ate the stalest items first) he outlined his programme. They would start before the light was entirely gone and make for the southern section of the reserve. He believed that a main road ran somewhere in that direction. And there was a railway somewhere near. In point of fact, they had heard hoarse whistles and the far-off clang of bells during the afternoon. The trouble was going to be at the bridges, he said. If they came to any considerable stream, they must follow it or find some means of crossing. He was an expert on such things, she gathered, and had evaded several unhappy experiences by a careful avoidance of bridges. As far as he could understand, they would 'fetch up' in the morning midway between Farnham and Aldershot.

Night was coming down when, with the motor rug rolled and fastened horse-collar fashion about his shoulder, he led the way. The wood was deeper than she thought. Between tree-tops she saw the thin crescent of a new moon … the harsh shriek of an owl at hand made her jump involuntarily.

'Made me jump, too,' he comforted her.

They were descending all the time, and this worried him a little. Most abruptly their progress was stopped by a high wire fence. The wood's natural boundary was beyond this, for the wire ran irregularly from tree to tree. Searching the ground, he found a piece of branch wood suitable for the purpose, and prised up the lower strand of wire.

'You can slip under – keep very close to the ground and make yourself thin!'

She got under with only a slight mishap. One of the sharp barbs caught the old coat which she insisted she should wear, and ripped a narrow strip.

'You'll be real tramp in a week,' he said. 'Rags and tatters – I must hunt up a tomato can for you!'

By some miracle he himself wriggled under without a scratch.

' "Let caution mark the way",' he quoted, dropping his voice. 'The road is nearer than I thought.'

Nearer indeed. From the thicket-like density of the wood they came suddenly within a few yards of the open, and a road bright with the lights of stationary motor cars.

' ... the woodman said he saw 'em go into Mr Murphy's preserve. Don't let anybody move till we get the signal from the fellers on the other side of the park.'

A tall, red-faced farmer was addressing a select and approving audience. Even as he spoke there came the sound of a shot from beyond the woods.

'Get your lights ready, boys, and don't shoot the young lady.'

They came surging up the bank to where a petrified October stood gripping the tramp's sleeve in terror.

VIII

'Back! Under the wire ... I'll go first.'

Before she reached the fence he was under ... he dragged her through with some violence. She heard another rent appear in her coat.

'Left ... hurry. They don't know about the wire.'

Evidently the party had halted for another reason.

'Spread out! You go right along to the corner. Mr Loamer – where's Mr Loamer? ... Oh, Mr Loamer, you stay with us.'

The corner? There would be an angle to the fence, and the

confines of the estate must be fairly near.

'Run!' he said under his breath, and she obeyed.

The right-angle fence appeared as unexpectedly as its fellow. Peering through, Robin saw that the roadway was deserted. He yanked up the lower strand and the girl slipped under. She held the wire less efficiently whilst he followed.

'Nothing – my coat wouldn't show a new tear.'

The man ordered to the corner must have obeyed with some reluctance. He was nowhere in sight. The two made to the right, keeping by the side of the road and walking in single file. From the wood came the sound of a shot and then another; there followed a fusillade. She saw that he was shaking with laughter.

'They will kill one another, and I shall be blamed,' he said, and was almost prophetic.

Two specks of light showed ahead of them. They lay flat on the side of the road until the car passed.

'We had better keep to the verge,' he said, and explained that the ancient word for the borders of a road was 'slang.' 'Gipsies used to camp on the slang – gipsies and wandering tinkers with a queer language of their own. And "slang" has passed into the vocabulary as all queer languages.'

He was oddly informative and at the most unlikely moments.

They walked over a mile before they came to a by-road. Private tracks there were, leading to gloomy farm buildings; once a big dog leapt out at them from an open gate. Robin whistled, and the dog came to his side and was with difficulty persuaded to go to his home again.

They were within a few yards of the side road when October whispered:

'Are you sure we are not being followed?'

He looked back.

'I didn't think we were; why?'

'I don't know – I'm nervous. I suppose. But I thought – '

They turned at this minute and he waved her on and, crouching down by the corner of the fence that bounded the main road, looked back. He remained for a few minutes before he joined the girl.

'I saw nobody – did you?'

She hesitated.

'No – I'm not sure. I thought I saw somebody walking on the side of the road. It may have been imagination.'

Less than a mile away was a railroad. They saw a brilliantly lighted train moving across the landscape.

'There is a level crossing at the end of this road, I suppose,' mused Robin. 'We might take to the railway track, but I've a notion that wouldn't help us very much. We'd probably land in the very place we wish to avoid.'

The plan was to cross the track and find a road on the far side that ran parallel. That which they now trudged did not run straight to the railroad, they found. Half way down there there was a sharp elbow, and in the crook of it were two high gates flanked by tall pillars that led to a drive and eventually, as he supposed, to a house hidden behind the high clipped hedges that lined the fence and flanked the drive. As he stopped to make an inspection a dog barked furiously, but evidently it was leashed.

But a bigger danger than dogs threatened. As they stood, October saw that she was casting a long, dim shadow on the ground. The man had seen it, too, and looked round. At the far end of the road two motor lamps showed and they were growing in brilliance every fraction of a second.

Robin made a swift survey. There was no cover of any kind: it was impossible that, passing them, the motorists could miss seeing them, and in that bright light there could be no question but that they would be identified. He saw an iron ring dangling from the gate, turned it, and, as a heavy iron latch came up, the big gate moved open.

October needed no instructions to follow: she had become inured to furtiveness and was inside the gate almost as soon as he. He fastened the gate again ... the dog was barking furiously. So close was the car that there was light enough to see the gaps that offered shelter. They had to crawl on hands and knees before they rolled over, completely hidden. The machine had stopped: somebody got down and, walking to the gate, flung it open with a crash. From the direction of the invisible house a man's voice asked:

'Is that you, Dick?'

'Yes. Sorry I'm late – Bill, did you hear the shooting?'

The man walked from the house up the drive to meet them, his feet scrunching pleasantly on the gravel.

'Eh? Shooting? Yes, I thought I heard something. Dog was barking like mad. What is the trouble?'

'That dam' tramp – the fellow that killed the girl. They got him on Murphy's land – Murphy is trying to look as if he enjoyed having his birds shot over in September! Some of these fellows started in to blaze away at one another. Nobody killed – that's the wonder. I'll get the car inside ... sorry I'm late ... '

His voice receded: evidently he was going to the car. There was a harsh purr, the machine turned cautiously into the drive and somebody clanged the gate behind it.

'Let my man come out and put it away ... leave it, Dick.'

There was a chuckle, a snap of steel.

'Best lock the gears whilst that bird is around. He lifted a car last night – found it up on Quarry Hill ... eh? Wait, I'll get my suitcase.'

'Come on' – impatiently. 'I'll send Hawkins for it.'

Sounds of two pairs of feet on gravel ... silence as they crossed the grass floor on a lawn.

'Get out – quick as you can,' Robin whispered. She had never seen him quite as excited. 'Walk along towards the railway ... and wait.'

October obeyed, wriggling out under the hedge – a terribly difficult exit this proved to be, for the car lights had been extinguished and she could not see the providential gap through which they had come.

She lifted the latch noiselessly and stepped into the road. She thought that the car steal of the night before was to be repeated, and it might have been but for those locked gears. The current was also locked off, but he should have made a short circuit under the bonnet and overcome that difficulty. The gears defied him ...

She turned to the right as she went out, and had walked a hundred yards when a doubt assailed her. The house had been on the left: she was going back the way she had come. Or wasn't she? Standing irresolutely for a moment, she considered. She saw the lights of a winking train as it passed through a belt of trees. Of course ...

She had started to run, when she saw the men. They stood one on each side of the road, motionless pillars of black ... but men. Her heart was thumping painfully; for an instant she was breathless. Robin must be warned: they had been followed.

She walked rapidly along the centre of the road, and they crossed to intercept her.

'Excuse me, Miss.'

It was Red Beard. She would have detected his voice amongst a thousand.

'Good-night,' said October, and would have gone on, but he threw out his hand and she found her arm gripped painfully.

'Goin' far, Miss?'

'No ... to Mr – to the house. Please let me go – or I'll call for – my brother.'

'Didn't know she had any brother, d'you, Lenny? Thought she was just one lone li'l orphan. Hey, where's that hobo friend of yourn?'

'I don't know what you mean.' She spoke loudly. Robin could hear. And then a panic seized her. Suppose he heard and came? These two men were after him; one threw knives ...

'What's the matter – nobody's goin' to hurt you, are they, Lenny?'

He invariably appealed to Lenny, and as a general rule Lenny said nothing. He bent over past her and whispered into the ear of his companion.

'Uh huh,' grunted Lenny, 'thasso.'

'You come along back to your husband, ma'am,' said Red Beard. 'I guess we're mighty poor kind of hicks after runnin' around with that swell friend of yours, but you better stick along of us, hey, Lenny?'

All the time she was conscious of a tense alertness in him; he was like a man who expected attack from some quarter, he knew not whence. Then she saw the gun in his hand – sensed it rather, for the night was very dark; the crescent moon had slid down from the sky and only the stars gave light.

'Come along.' His grip of her arm did not relax: he was sidling. Lenny made no pretence that he was not walking backwards.

Starlight, faint and ghostly, was reflected back in the knife he carried between finger and thumb.

'What are you scared of?' she asked. 'And must you walk like a crab? – If he shoots you, you will fall on me.'

She heard the quick catch of his breath, and then he laughed softly, but not heartily.

'Tha's good! Heard that, Lenny? I guess your friend's somewhere around, ma'am? There's a bunch handy that wants to get acquainted with him. Ain't there, Lenny?'

'Thasso,' said Lenny.

'Got a gun, ain't he, ma'am? I'll bet – '

'Watch out!'

For the life of her she could not resist the mischievous inclination. He jumped sidways with an oath. For an instant she was free, but he clawed at her.

'Say ... what's this funny stuff, Missis Tramp? What's the idea? I guess we're laughin' at you, ain't we, Lenny? Funny stuff ... '

He was loud and angry. Thereafter they progressed much more quickly, but neither Red Beard nor the silent Lenny kept their heads still. Every two steps, one glance back.

'We'll get *him*, don't worry, ma'am. He's around, that's all we want to know. There's two men guardin' the crossin' anyway. I guess before mornin' we'll be takin' you down to the morgue an' saying' "Pick yours, ma'am," hey, Lenny?'

'Thasso,' said Lenny.

'What are you in real life,' she asked. 'Just thieves or merely American gunmen?'

'Say – '

'Gunmen, I suppose,' she nodded. 'Mr – my friend said they're cheapest in Chicago.'

Red Beard had his civic pride. Chicago was his home town.

He developed a spluttering obscurity of speech.

'Listen, you ... what's good enough for me's good enough for ... say, what's the matter with you anyway ... Cheap! I like that, hey, Lenny? What's cheaper'n a hobo's girl ... huh!'

They had reached the post road; there was a thrilling spectacle revealed. Quite near them, cars were packed bonnet to tail. The ground rose gently to one side of the road, apparently no man's land, for the sloping ground beyond was unfenced. A fire was burning, a regular camp fire that lit the trees picturesquely.

IX

Mr Loamer sat there, an aloof and somewhat grotesque figure, in his frockcoat pitiably soiled, and trousers that no longer creased. His large red face was unshaven and he blinked from group to group with unseeing eyes. The world was crashing about George Loamer's ears. Of a sudden, by his own volition, he had passed into the public gaze, and was aching to recover his obscurity. In his handsome office he could plan and manipulate and manoeuvre vast schemes, and none was the wiser save his confidential clerk. From Market Chase he could pull strings and set the wheels of a well-ordered system moving. But here he was out of his element, unable to control or propitiate the honest fury he had aroused in the bosoms of the sympathetic populace.

The police had been enquiring: there had arrived two men from Scotland Yard who wanted to know all about his marriage, where the ceremony had been performed, the circumstances under which his ward had changed her plans for a Continental tour and undertaken this new and enormous responsibility. How they knew of the tour, he could not guess. One had gone prying into the recesses of Four Beeches and had discovered in its untenanted wing a bedroom recently occupied. Who had been staying there? Where were they now?

In a cold sweat of fear Mr Loamer had contradicted himself, and then in a panic he had wired for that masterful mother of his, and she had come laden with reproach, a nettle of a woman who stung at every contact. He sat by the fire, biting his nails fretfully. If he could only get October back ... if she were dead ... yes, it were better she were dead ...

He looked up at this point, his scorched eyes staring to one side of the blazing wood. The red-bearded man he knew ... And then he came to his feet.

'October!' he gasped, and was uncertain how further to proceed.

There she stood, gravely surveying him, an object of interest to threescore pairs of startled eyes. He saw the ragged, mud stained dress, the torn coat, and blinked at her again.

'October! My – my dear!'

He put out his shaking hand, but hers were behind her back.

She had already made up her mind as to the course she would follow. With her capture she thought the search would end, and Robin the tramp would have an opportunity for escape.

'I'll go back with you,' she said, very distinctly and slowly.

George Loamer looked left and right in mute appeal. He wanted – how very badly he needed – the presence of his mother at that moment. Suppose October told the truth? He had not even a lie to counter her.

'All right ... October ... we'll go along.'

He was awkward, trembling, in a terror lest she accused him. At the moment he imagined that she was privy to all the unpleasant secrets that his quaking heart held. That she would presently denounce him as a bankrupt and worse.

He looked round fearfully. The two quiet men from Scotland Yard were not there, and with a sudden courage he gripped her arm and hurried her down the slope to his waiting car.

Red Beard? She strained her eyes towards the road. There were several men there, but Red Beard was not among them. That interminable journey! October curled up in one corner of the car, George Loamer in the other. She woke from a doze as the machine glided through the gates of Four Beech Farm. The room she had left was unchanged. The house smelt stale –

worse than the earthy kitchen at the Shepherd's cottage. That heavy Georgian furniture; the solemn faced clock in the wide hall – there ought by rights to be a hook in the ceiling whereon a broken heart could make a swift, sad, merciful transition to a land where tramps like angels wander hand in hand through scented woods. Not love ... it wasn't love. Hero worship! She fell into a paroxysm of laughter. And then the door clanged behind her, and the laugh died on her lips as the stout Martha, oily faced and menacing, her plump hands folded, confronted her.

'You've got a lot to laugh about.'

Martha had lived under the shadow of terror for twenty-four hours and her voice was tremulous.

'What lies you've told I don't know.'

'That will do.' It was Loamer's harsh voice that interrupted the flow of reproach. 'What did you tell that damned tramp?'

October was very calm now.

'I told him nothing,' she said.

He was peering at her through narrowed lids. The change in his appearance in the two days was remarkable. His smooth face had sunk into strange hollows and wrinkles.

'Did you tell him about – ' – he found a difficulty in speaking – 'the old man?'

'Where is he?' she asked quickly.

'Never mind where he is. Did you tell him?'

'I told him nothing,' she answered briefly.

He was searching her face and did not speak for a long time. When he did, it was to tell her that they were leaving in the morning for London. Then he turned to Martha.

'See if you can keep her this time,' he said harshly, and went up the broad stairway to his room and she heard the slam of his door.

Martha led her into her stuffy little sitting-room and pointed majestically to a chair. October sat meekly, noting she had interrupted Martha's supper, for a coffee cup stood on the table, and had evidently been poured full before her arrival.

'You'd better get what you can to eat, and then you go to bed, young lady,' she said. 'You'll sleep in my room to-night.'

She handed the cup to October with a gesture of disparagement. October sipped the hot fluid thoughtfully. Perhaps it wasn't true about the guard at the railway crossing. A lie would come naturally to Red Beard. And Robin was cautious – almost he was like one of the wild creatures of the forest. He could see things in the dark, things invisible to her. So the shepherd hanged himself on the hook after all. It was nothing to smile about, but she smiled, and Martha, who watched her every expression, felt her anger rising.

'Glad you can grin!'

'Grinning – was I?' She was almost penitent; Martha had never seen her that way before. 'I'm sorry; I was thinking of ... things entirely different. I suppose I must stay here? Couldn't I have another room?'

A suggestion on which the woman had very emphatic views.

It was at that moment that there was a knocking at the front door. Martha got up with a frown and disappeared.

To and fro October rocked, her cheek on her palm. Over the back of a chair her tattered, bark-torn coat was hanging; it was lovely to see. Almost every stain and rent could be identified with some stage of her – of their adventure.

The door opened slowly and Martha came in, her face twitching. Behind her came a tall man in evening dress. His soft white shirt was like snow, his black tie was most correct; his trousers were an inch too short, and a gap of shirt showed between his waistcoat and the top of his pants. He had a stubbly moustache and sidewhiskers, and a pair of horn-rimmed pince-nez, a little askew, were on his nose.

'Mr Sullivan, from Scotland Yard,' he gruffly introduced himself. 'Is this the young lady?'

As he indicated October, four inches of shirt-cuff shot out. The sleeves of his coat were a little short.

October gazed, fascinated.

'I came by special – from London,' said Mr Sullivan. 'Young lady, you're under arrest!'

October nodded. She had no questions to ask.

'Get your coat – have you any food in the house?' This to Martha. The lady nodded; the right words would not come.

Only she gazed helplessly at the door, expecting, hoping for the apparition of her master.

Upstairs in his room, George Loamer was changing both his clothes and his plans. He would leave by car for London that night – in London were banks and offices where steamship tickets could be bought. The end was in sight.

'Cheese, bread, biscuits.' Mr Sullivan's eyes fell on the coffee-pot. 'Coffee. We have a long journey.'

'Under arrest?' Martha found her voice quakily.

'Under arrest,' said Mr Sullivan solemnly. 'Contravention of Section twenty-nine.'

Martha vanished into the kitchen. She returned in a remarkably short space of time with a basket loaded with odd things.

'Have you a bottle – a large bottle?'

She nodded dumbly, returned from the kitchen with a bottle – a large bottle. Gravely Mr Sullivan half-filled it from the coffee-pot; added milk. He took two large handfuls of sugar and solemnly put them into the pocket of his smoking jacket. His gravity was almost depressing.

'Arrested? Is anybody else ... ' Martha's voice quavered.

Mr Sullivan regarded her severely for the space of a second, then he took up the coat that was hanging over the chair.

'Yours?'

October nodded. She was on her feet now.

'Come,' he said, and took two cups from the table. He had the bottle in one hand, the basket in the other; an apple fell out: he stooped and picked it up.

'Screak!'

A back seam of the jacket parted under the strain, and a white slither of shirt showed.

October went obediently, meekly. Outside the gate stood a car, its engine running. 'Chug, chug, CHUG!' Every third 'chug' was more explosive than its fellows. She scrambled into a machine which was without dignity.

The car rattled wheezily through Ashleigh and came again to the well-remembered road. October sighed luxuriously.

'Robin, I think you're wonderful!' she breathed.

PART TWO

I

Some twenty miles away a distracted and wrathful young man was telephoning to the police.

' … a brown leather suitcase. R.T. on both sides … Eh? I *told* you – hours ago I told you. Listen, write it down, will you: a brown leather suitcase. It was strapped on the back of my car. It had an evening-dress suit, a safety-razor outfit, and – well, the usual things. And a suit of pyjamas.'

Robin grew conversational as the car jogged along.

'The pyjamas were rather superfluous – I chucked them into a field. I'm sorry now; you could have worn the pants as a scarf. And that razor … my heavens, it *hurt*!'

The car had been gathered from the parking place near the camp fire. It was the end machine – nobody had seen it go.

'But the shaving … cold water and no glass, and this face of mine!'

'Did you see me taken away?' she asked.

'From the Boy Scouts – yes. As a matter of fact, you passed me. What really happened?'

She told him about Red Beard, but this was no news to him. He had seen Red Beard.

'I guessed that you had gone in the wrong direction when I didn't see you. I stopped to loot the suitcase. I'm wearing silk undies – I feel royal!'

She asked nothing. When they came to the side road where the case had been acquired he turned down. As they passed the house where the wronged owner of a good dress suit was expressing his views about the police and police methods, he waved a silent salute to the author of his comfort.

Red Beard had only half lied. At the crossing was a policeman. As they passed, he shouted.

'You haven't seen – '

The rest of the sentence was inaudible.

'Good night!' roared Robin as they bumped across the track.

'I could have wished something less conspicuous than a dress suit,' he said, 'but finders can't choose. And I feel like the Prince of Wales. Besides, as we're doing our walking by night the costume is appropriate. You weren't frightened when I appeared?'

'I knew you – of course I knew you,' she scoffed.

'I thought you would – hullo!' He jerked his head round to look back.

'What was it?' she asked.

'A man lying beside the road – hiding, I think. You don't know which way Red Whiskers went after he left the Wolf Cubs?'

She had not seen his going. Robin considered all the possibilities.

He guessed I was making for the railway,' he said at last. 'Perhaps he thought I had already gone on. I wonder what the Managing Director thinks about it all.' This was the title he had adopted for Loamer's mother.

She could advance no postulation.

'Looks like a cross-road ahead,' he said. 'Suppose we turn down, shut off the lights and eat. I had to abandon the grub and I'm starving.'

The cross-road was, it seemed, the main road, not a spot for lingering. A few miles along this highway, they found a likely lane and a suitable halting ground. There was a glow in the western sky – faint but distinguishable. He suspected the presence of a large town.

'Farnham can't be very far away,' he said.

She was not very hungry but she ate to keep him in countenance.

'If we could hide the car you could sleep in it,' he said. 'There is a skin blanket of some kind in the back. I'd give a thousand pounds for a line to the habits and customs of the local tribe! There must be any number of old barns that nobody ever looks into. You knew me, eh?'

He seemed pleased at this and reverted to her recognition again.

'Loamer may go to the police – he's in rather a desperate position.'

She put down the cup from which she had been drinking.

'What is your crime?' she asked. 'I know that you are a burglar and a car thief, but what have you done that is *seriously* wrong?'

He laughed as he got down and cranked up the car, but he offered no explanation.

They rattled on for a mile or so and reached a three-way cross-road. He took the centre way and they came presently to a gaunt-looking building, very square and ugly, that stood within a few yards of the road. The wire fence that indicated the boundary was sagging and in places missing. One of the finds he made when he searched the car was an electric torch, and with this in his hand he went exploring.

The foreground was littered with iron barrels, Rank grass grew through and about the debris. There, in the neglect and desolation, was unmistakable evidence of ruin. He saw that the window glass was broken; on the black door that was squarely in the middle of the building was a half-obliterated tramp sign written with chalk. He puzzled over this sign for a time: it might be a private signature revealing the identity of the writer, or a piece of general information. Was it 'not safe'?

Picking his way carefully through the rubbish, he rounded a corner of the building and continued. At the far end he came upon a one-storied annexe built on to the main structure. He could imagine this had once been an office of the long-departed occupants. There was a small door and he tried this, never expecting that it would open. To his surprise, it yielded readily – too readily: somebody was pulling from the inside, and he stepped back quickly, pulling the gun from his pocket.

In the light of his lamp he saw a very old man. His rags were indescribably foul, his face had not known soap and water for weeks. White bearded and bald, he stood, one hand on the door, blinking at the light.

And then he spoke, not loudly but in an undertone, as though he were afraid of disturbing somebody's sleep. But half of the words and phrases he used were Greek to the listener.

'I am afraid I can't understand you,' he said.

The old man looked back into the room and stepped out, closing the door very gently.

'My mistake entirely.' The voice was that of an educated man. 'I did not see you well. The light ... disconcerting. Hum!'

He peered forward shortsightedly.

'Hum! I see you have dressed for dinner. The fashion has changed considerably. A soft shirt, for example, was regarded as – er – déclassé. But fashions change.'

His grimy hand felt the texture of the coat.

'It is rather interesting ... hum!' He shook his bald head. 'Let me see ... it was in '90 or a little later that I last ... hum!'

Robin was startled alike by the accent and the substance of the old man's speech.

'It was before the trouble about the money,' said the old gentleman, reminiscent, 'and long before the Apparition. That came to me in – er – Hampshire, or possibly it was London ... in – I cannot tell you the date.'

He spoke pleasantly, in the way of an old man retailing his reminiscences. He had been a professor of anatomy, he remarked casually – before the trouble with the money and long before the Apparition and He.

'Who is He?' asked Robin.

The old man nodded towards the door.

'He thinks I am mad ... because of the ... Appearance. I have tried to explain that I have gifts not vouchsafed to every man. But I can sympathise with a sceptic. I should have laughed ten, twenty years ago ... hum!'

Robin thought it was time to ask vital questions.

'A car? Let me think!' The old man smoothed his shiny pate. 'There is a shed behind – nobody comes to the studio ... as they call it. It was occupied by a moving picture – er – maker. I am glad you came.'

'Why?'

'I am glad you came,' repeated the old man. 'The Apparition ... I am not sure that I understood her. She is usually so explicit. But to-night ... nebulous, indefinite. Naturally one would not like to fall into error. Was it not perhaps that my own sense of personal grievance ... He gave me rather a bad beating. Look!'

He pointed to his mouth: it was swollen and cut.

'Is this somebody you are travelling with?'

The ancient nodded seriously.

'His name I do not know. Harry they call him.' He glanced nervously at the door. 'I will show you the shed,' he said, and went ahead. 'We have been together for eight years – longer perhaps. He – er – looked after me. I find him useful. But he is very cruel ... hum!'

The 'shed' was a lean-to, but if, as the old man said, this disused studio was a place that nobody visited, the shelter was on the side of the building where it was least likely to be observed.

'This is a favourite "sleep" for the confraternity.' The visitor gathered what he meant. 'But I am afraid we have the best place. But of course you would not wish to sleep here?'

Robin broke it to him that he would, and the old man did not seem surprised.

'Are you alone? No – there is a store in a corner of the grounds. I have not been there myself, but I understand that it is comfortable in dry weather.'

He would have shown the way, but Robin declined his assistance and they returned to the front of the one-storeyed building to find that He was waiting in the open for him. A giant of a man, almost a head taller than Robin.

'Hey! What's this, Jesse ... Leavin' the door open, you little – '

His language was not delicate. Robin showed his lamp on to the ground. It gave enough light to see the stranger. Poorly but not uncomfortably dressed, well fed, burly ... there all that could be said favourably of his appearance finished. A low receding forehead, a gross button of a nose and a huge chin;

eyes as small, as dark, and as close-set as a monkey's.

The old man addressed him as 'O' and was pitifully anxious to propitiate him.

'Get in and make that bed again, you little swine!' He lifted his foot; the bald old man dodged the kick with remarkable agility.

In the light, 'O' had seen the white expanse of dress shirt and was plainly troubled.

'I'm taking him to London – he's not right in his head.'

'You're his keeper?' asked the astonished Robin.

'Yes – that's so. He's got a fancy for walking. He'd attract a lot of attention if we went by train. And he's scared of cars.'

'Has he any relations?' asked Robin.

'No – and not much money. We'd have got lodgings only the little devil won't go near a village. We have to humour 'em. Good-night, mister.'

It was the moment to put 'O' right. Robin explained.

'Sleeping here? You're mad, too! Anyway, there's no room.' The note of deference was gone from his voice. 'What's the idea?'

'I'm staying here, that's all,' said Robin shortly and turned away.

He expected the man to follow, but he made no movement. Very briefly he explained to October what the position was.

'I don't think we can get the car much farther,' he said. 'The tank is nearly empty, but I may be able to scrounge a tin to-morrow.'

He drove the car over the ruts and furrows, surmounted mysterious heaps of refuse and backed it into the shelter. Then they went in search of the corner store. It was a small windowless building that had evidently been used as a sleeping place before. Door there was none; the floor was bare, not even a sack had been left. The one-time whitewashed walls were covered with pencilled inscriptions by former occupants. Some of them were translatable and others unprintable. There were also drawings, but he dropped his light quickly from these.

'You had better try the floor,' he said, and laid the cushions and rug he had brought from the car in one corner.

He heard her whisper, and looking up, saw the giant form of 'O' silhouetted in the doorway. Robin walked out of the hut.

'Want anything?' he asked.

'Who's the skirt?'

Robin's light flashed full on the animal face of the man. He shaded his eyes and saw the gun in the other hand.

'Go back where you belong.'

'Hi! hi! what's the matter with you ... !'

'Get!'

The big man shambled off into the darkness; his curses came back with undesirable clearness.

'Who is he?'

'O,' said Robin laconically. 'Or "nought" – he's nothing.'

One cushion sufficed him. He planted it in the doorway, pulled a rubber sheet round him and, with his back to the wall, dozed. It was a long time before October fell into a fitful sleep. She must have awakened a dozen times, but whenever she turned or stretched, she saw a movement at the door and knew that he was awake. Finally she sat up, pushed back her hair and yawned.

'Did it waken you?' asked the voice from the doorway.

'It? What was it? I heard nothing.'

'I've an idea that my poor lunatic friend is getting a beating – for two cents I'd go over.'

What he meant, as she knew, was that, but for the necessity of guarding her sleep, he would have gone.

She yawned, got up on her feet, pulling on her shoes, and joined him. His head was bent, listening. From somewhere in the grounds came the sound of weeping, a thin, weak crying like a child's.

'Poor old Baldy!' he said softly.

She asked him what he meant and he told her of the old man called 'Jesse'. Even then she did not associate him with the nightmare vision she had seen at Four Beeches.

'I suspect he is a slave. Some of the old hands have these poor devils to fetch and carry for them. Baldy is one of such.'

He told her nothing of the money or the apparition or the great University where Baldy had lectured to students who were now great doctors driving in their pretentious limousines. The tale was harrowing enough, and he was not past being harrowed himself.

The weeping ceased. She brought her blanket, put it round her shoulders and sat with him. He had had 'forty winks', he said, and anyway he did not require much sleep, boasting, that he had once kept awake for three days and night.

'Where was this?' she asked, and he answered vaguely that it was in Europe, and did not think it worth while explaining that an intensive enemy bombardment of his trench had been a contributory cause to his wakefulness.

Just as the first pale light came into the east, they heard another cry. An 'Ow!' hoarse and startling. Nothing followed. Robin moved uneasily. He could see the angle of the building now – the after side of the office. Then he rose.

'I really must go over, I am afraid,' he said. 'Do you mind? You will be quite safe here.'

'Shall I come with you?'

'Yes ... perhaps it would be better.'

The morning was chilly; he helped her into the beloved coat and they stepped out side by side.

They rounded the corner and stopped before the door, listening. No sound came from inside the 'office'. He motioned her back and pushed the door gently. As it opened a little he listened again. Sharp as his ears were, he could detect no sound of breathing. The atmosphere was thick. He made a grimace and moved the door wide open.

Still no sound. He could have switched on the light, but he did not wish to disturb them – they must sleep soundly if fresh air did not rouse their shivering protests. The room was inkily dark. He took one cautious step, and then his foot slipped on something and he lost his balance. Down he came sprawling.

II

It was soft and wet. His hands were covered with a warm, sticky fluid. Up to his feet he came in a second and flashed down the lamp on the face of the man called 'O'. He looked, petrified with horror, then his lamp searched for Jesse who was once a professor of anatomy and saw Apparitions. The old man was not there.

Robin stooped and wiped his hand on the man's coat, then he backed out. October was waiting, a dim figure in the grey dimness.

'Was he … ?'

Then she saw the white shirt-front.

'Blood!' she whispered. 'Is the old man hurt?'

He shook his head.

'The other – ?'

'Dead – sorry.'

He sent the light round its limited range. There was no sign of the old man who spoke such good English. Perhaps he was already with the Apparition that came to him some nights and leered and pointed him his duty.

They went back to the little store and gathered rug and cushions.

'We must get away from here – quick,' he said, carrying the equipment to the car. 'The poor old beggar! Professor of anatomy! I should say so!'

When he cranked up the car, the noise of it sounded deafening. Nobody could live on the earth and not hear it.

'I don't know how far we can run on a quart of juice,' he said, 'but we'll go as far as we can.'

They came out on to the road and turned in the direction they had been heading when the car had stopped before the studio. The light was still faint – hardly distinguishable from night. Patches of white mist lay in the hollows, and when they descended a sharp dip they ran into a fog that continued a surprising time.

Now they were climbing a road that was cut in the side of a bare hill. The engines began to make spluttering noises, the machine went on in jerks. Near to the top, it went dead. He pulled the brake, and, getting down, walked to the crest. From here the road ran gently downhill.

He came back and told her, and together, with great labour, they pushed the machine to the far side of the ridge. Here they sat down and regained their breath.

'Can't you take off your shirt?' she asked anxiously. 'It is – dreadful! And your hands ... '

She looked round for water but there was no spring here.

'Couldn't I buy you some clothes?' she asked suddenly.

He put his hand in his pocket and when he withdrew it she saw two shillings on his palm.

'Buy me anything up to two shillings,' he said. She had no money. Her wrist-watch might have a selling value, but it could not be a high one.

'Great Moses!'

She followed the direction of his startled eyes. He was looking backwards: the hill commanded a view of the road along which they had come ... big white billows of smoke were rising from the studio ... she saw the red and yellow flames lick up and vanish.

'On fire – he did it ... the old hero!'

She knew that he was talking of Baldy. Then his face fell.

'That is going to call together all the police in miles,' he said, 'and they will find "O" – both parts of him.'

Without another word he stripped off his coat and shirt. Underneath was the silk which made him feel royal. He made a bundle of waistcoat and shirt, looked longingly at the petrol tank and finally stuffed them under one of the back cushions.

'Let us glide,' he said.

The car went smoothly downhill. He might have got a movement for his engine, but he was reserving this for a final run on the level.

'You must be dreadfully cold – have the rug around your shoulders,' said October, but though he was shivering he refused the offer.

There was a little township ahead of them. The inevitable farm lorry appeared in the road. Robin made a signal and the driver, a sleepy and disgruntled youth, stopped.

'Yes, I've got petrol, but – '

Robin bargained and lied. He had a manner with him that combined hauteur and good humour. He sought for the young man's weak spot and found it.

'This young lady is my daughter – she's rushing to meet the 6.15. Queer thing is that I came along without money – look!'

Two shillings displayed up a broad palm look very few shillings.

'That's not enough for a tin,' said the young man, one eye on October. 'I'd get the sack. Still – '

He had a can that was near full. The exchange was effected.

'Where you from? Not Ashleigh? They caught that tramp last night an' run him in. Over Mr Murphy's estate ... *you* know. He poisoned a feller an' got his wife away – she's dead, too.'

'Glory be!' said Robin. 'I must tell her – I must tell my daughter.'

A few miles further along a motor fire-engine came rocking past, smothered with dust.

'We are getting near to civilisation,' said Robin. 'This is where we go very slow.'

He had hardly spoken before he heard the hideous shriek of a motor horn behind. He thought it was the fire float and took no notice. Again the angry yelp. Looking back, he saw a car and, drawing into the side waved it on.

'It's very early for traffic – ' he began, and then the car drew abreast and passed. The man at the wheel was big-featured and unshaven. From the heap of furs by his side protruded the dead white face of a lady with a large Roman nose. For a second their eyes met ... she spoke to the man at her side and he half turned his head, straightened it again and swerved before the little machine.

'What a nerve!' said Robin.

It was all over in two seconds, the exchange of glances, the passing. The machine ahead accelerated, became a dim form showing between rolling clouds of dust, and was gone.

'Mrs Loamer!' said October.

'And Georgie,' he said.

At the next cross road he stopped and examined the wheel tracks. The diamond-pattern tyres had gone due north; he took the westerly road and was sorry. So many were the houses hereabouts that he guessed he was approaching the suburbs of a large town. There were cars and people on the road – people who were interested in a man dressed simply in a dress coat and silk vest. And the spirit was running low. A garage was opening, and he stopped the car before its doors. But the man who was opening up was an assistant and had no authority to lend petrol.

'Would you like to buy this handsome car?' blandly.

The garage hand regarded this suggestion as a humourless joke. Then he said something.

'Cut yourself, ain't you?'

He was looking curiously at Robin's hand.

'Could you drive a car like that and not cut yourself?' he demanded.

October came to the rescue.

'My uncle – has left home without money and we have to get on to Aldershot. Would you lend us some spirit if I left my watch with you – or would you buy it?'

The garage man took the watch and smiled cleverly. He was not, said the smile, the kind of man who would succumb to the lure of fake jewellery. With disparagement written large upon his homely face bearing relics of yesterday's toil, he weighed the little gold timepiece in his hand.

'Worth about ten shillings,' he said. 'You can buy 'em cheaper, but ten shillings'd be fair.'

The watch had cost thirty pounds, a year before.

'Make it a pound,' said October courageously.

The young man half shook his head. He had a girl for whose birthday he had designed an expensive present – and an expensive present is one that is just a little more than you can afford. And it was a nice watch. It had been worn and yet remained gold.

'Ten shillings is all that I could give you for that watch.'

A brilliant idea came to October.

'You shall have that little watch for five shillings and a suit of clothes,' she said, with solemn earnestness.

He was staggered, but the bargaining faculties of the man were stirred. He had a suit ... a very old suit ...

'Wait,' he said.

Near to the garage was the tiniest wooden house she had ever seen. It looked to be rather a large tool chest, yet into this he disappeared. When he came out, garments were hanging over his arm. October took them one by one and examined them critically.

'They're not Savile Row, are they?' she asked, and he, who had taken a correspondence course in the French language, thought she had introduced a foreign idiom and answered 'Oui.'

With five shillings' worth of petrol in the tank, and the suit neatly folded on the back seat, the car sped on its way.

'He's very slight, not to say skinny,' said Robin ominously. 'I'm going to *bulge*!'

They were now in a more sparsely peopled country; farms were fewer, there were clumps of trees and fast-running little streams. They followed the course of one of these until they came to a wooded glen.

He had abandoned food and covering, but had held fast to soap and towel – she had discovered this the night before, when the sugar with which he sweetened her coffee had imparted a faintly soapy flavour to an otherwise perfect refreshment.

'You go first,' he said, and produced the towel with a flourish.

Climbing down the steep bank to the stream, she made a hurried toilet and returned him apologetically a very damp towel. He had, he gravely informed her, a shirt. He used this to dry himself, washed the shirt in the stream and applied to his cheeks the safety razor. It was a groaning performance.

There came back to her a smart, youngish man with a moustache the ends of which had been soaped and twisted into spiky points. The vividly brown suit showed signs of wear and tear, but in many ways it fitted him better than the dress clothes he had abandoned. The crumpled dress collar had been straightened out, the black dress tie gave him an air of respectability.

'You look,' October summed up, 'rather like an unemployed undertaker.'

The shirt was spread on the engine to dry whilst they made a hasty meal and held a council of war. O's death had complicated matters, he said. The certain circulation of particulars and number of the stolen car, the appearance of Mr Sullivan at Four Beech Farm in a borrowed dress suit, and the swift recognition of Mrs Loamer were all bad enough. What would follow the discovery at the studio would be worse.

'But, my dear man, they can't say that you killed this wretched bully!' she protested.

They could and they might, he argued. He had been seen coming from the direction of the fire; the garage man had noted the blood on his hands.

'My only hope is the Managing Director – she's clever,' he said, and she was speechless with astonishment.

'But ... I thought she would have you arrested if she could? I understood that ... doesn't she hate you?'

He nodded, but did not reply, for his mouth was occupied with the half of a large apple.

'She loathes me,' he said. 'But the last thing she wishes is my arrest. She would strip her rings from her fingers, her diamonds from her ears, her king's-ransom pearls from her neck to prevent my arrest! That is her big worry. She will never forgive me for coming into the public eye. If you could get inside her soul you would find it like a tossing sea of despair. Poor old creature!'

October settled back in the corner of the car and moaned.

'I don't understand! What is the mystery? First you make me think that this wretched woman hates you, then you tell me she would sell her jewels – as I have done – to save you. Then you call her "poor old creature" as though she were your dearest friend!'

'I'm naturally mysterious,' he said modestly, but became serious immediately. 'The point is this: we're marked, and the car marks us. I don't know whether its lawful owner has already interviewed the police – it is rather early. But that risk can only be delayed a short while. Every garage will be notified, and our friend whose wardrobe I am representing is certain to betray us. The only hope in that direction is that he doesn't disclose the fact that he swopped clothes for your watch. Probably he won't. He will think that the watch has been stolen, and that if he tells the truth he will lose watch, shillings and suit. He will say that we filled up and went on.'

'What shall we do with the car?' she asked, impressed by his logic.

'Leave it – not here but near some town. You will have to leave your coat, too, I am afraid. That is positively trampish.'

He recovered his shirt. It was dry – in places. There were even yellow scorch marks. October made a suggestion. A thin branch of alder was broken off, and to its end the shirt was tied by its sleeves. There was hardly enough wind to stir the linen, but when the car started and the breeze caught the fluttering thing, it billowed out like an obese and shapeless sausage.

'An emblem of surrender and slightly conspicuous,' said Robin, glancing up, 'but ingenious.'

Fortunately the road was deserted, and the only man who saw this strange banner found a perfectly natural explanation for its presence. They had to strike their banner once for a farmer's cart, but by the time they came to the really dense traffic the shirt was dry. And they came up to the 'dense traffic' unexpectedly at the first cross road – two wagonettes, several cars, a little farm cart, crowded with young men and maidens in festal garb, they were all in sight when the machine, panting huskily, struggled over the top of a long steep hill.

'They are going to a fair,' said the girl, suddenly remembering.

Apparently the fair was an affair of some importance. Robin made up his mind quickly. Not to be going to the fair, would be, in the eyes of numerous travellers, both odd and noticeable. The best way to avoid attention was to drift with the stream. He turned with the tide, planted himself between a dilapidated joy wagon and a slow-moving and heavily loaded car, and kept his position.

The gaiety of the fair came out to meet them – stuff-roofed stalls where young men were eating quickly but solemnly; a little group, heads bent in a motionless scrum about a top-hatted man who was performing some miracle in the centre; another and larger group gathered round a small rostrum on which a bareheaded gentleman wearing a violent waistcoat and frock coat held a large pink-filled bottle in one hand and gesticulated with the other.

'We'll back in here,' said Robin.

They had reached the centre of the town; motor vehicles in every stage of beauty or decrepitude were parked at an angle to the pavement.

'Every town in the United Kingdom should have its name painted up in letters a mile high,' said Robin as he got down. 'We'll leave this bad baby here – I don't know a better place than a car park. Now where can I leave you?'

'Leave me?' she repeated in dismay.

He nodded.

'I want clothes for us both, a new car and information,' he said, 'and I shall get all these best if I work alone. By the way, I suppose you have never picked a pocket? That's a pity. I'm rather clumsy with my hands. We'll have to try another way.'

He left her outside a chemist's store with strict injunctions that she was not to move until he returned, and was soon lost to sight in the crowd. She stood for a long time watching the people. Immediately opposite where she stood was a big square stone building with a red shingled roof. Across its front in letters gilt and Gothic were the words 'Red Lion'. It was presumably the principal hotel, for on the narrow step before the building, and protected from the sun by a semi-circular veranda that had the appearance of a large eye-shade, was a line of chairs, occupied by shirt-sleeved men.

As she was looking, a long-bodied touring car drew up before the doors. It was covered with dust so that it was difficult to distinguish its colour, but the shape was familiar. It was the car that had passed them on the descent from the hill! More, it was the identical machine that she and Robin had left in the quarry forest. The woman with the Roman nose was not one of its three passengers, and Mr Loamer sat at the wheel.

First to descend was the passenger who had lolled at his ease behind. He opened his coat, shook off the dust and, standing up, removed his big goggles.

Red Beard!

Where was Robin? Her heart was beating furiously, and it was not from fear for herself. She withdrew her attention for a second and looked round for the echoing Lenny. He was nowhere in sight. When her eyes came back to Red Beard, he was apparently interested elsewhere. He had not followed the others into the hotel but strolled on, ignoring her. She wanted to follow, but Robin had told her to stay. And stay she must.

The crowd was increasing. Every minute brought a new contingent from the neighbouring towns and ... was she mistaken? ... more police. She saw a party of a dozen ride slowly down the street: they must have come some distance, for their horses were caked with dust, their flanks wet and heaving. And then a wagon drew up by the sidewalk and a dozen youngish men tumbled out. Police?

Surely more than was necessary to keep in order a few thousand law-abiding holiday makers, or to deal with the half-a-dozen manipulators of peas and walnut shells who lurked in secluded side streets to baffle and bleed the unwary.

She felt herself go white and red again. Robin's presence here was known, but that was not all. Something dreadful had happened.

She became conscious of a small and supernaturally clean boy with a collar that obviously irked him, who had appeared on the pavement. He stood, very ill at ease and uncertain, looking first at October, then at the store. In his hand he twisted and twirled a folded slip of paper. He edged nearer to her.

'Do you want me?' she asked in a low voice.

'You Mrs Loamer or somethin'?'

She almost snatched the note from his hand.

> Get to school far end of road. Walk on into country. Will endeavour pick you up. Police looking for me.

There was no signature. The note was written on a telegraph form.

She crumpled the paper in her hand and nodded to the boy. Evidently he expected no reward, for he did not linger.

She did not wait until the broad portals of Astor House had engulfed him before she joined that section of the leisurely throng that was moving in the direction of the school. To make absolutely sure that she had made no mistake she asked a woman loiterer.

Police ... everywhere!

Men obviously strangers to the town, who exchanged knowing glances with the uniformed men as they strolled passed them.

The school house was a building of glaring red brick, shingle-roofed, not to be missed. It was aloof from the town proper, nearer to a huddle of one-storeyed houses of microscopic dimensions that formed a suburb to the town and yet had an entity and a name of its own.

The road before the school was comparatively deserted except for the pedestrians and vehicles making for the town she had left. There was no sign of Robin.

'Walk on into country,' the note said, and she continued on her way. Soon the town of the fair (she never discovered its name) was behind her. On either side were fields dotted with sheaves of corn; farm buildings were numerous; ahead was the blue curve of hills. She stopped and sat down, staring back along the road. Except for the cars that had passed her there was nothing in sight.

A wagon of some kind was coming towards her, progressing with painful slowness. A diminutive man was driving – she thought at first he was a boy. The noise of the worn-out and patched-up engine was thunderous, even at a distance. As it came nearer it sounded like an artillery bombardment.

'Phut! Crash! Boom! Bang!' and through the major notes the counter melody of metallic tittering.

The driver was a middle-aged man with a wisp of iron-grey beard, and large rimless glasses on his nose. His face wore a look of fierce determination and labour, as though it were only the operations of his indomitable soul that kept the horrible machine in motion. It moved at a good walking pace; when it came near, the noise was deafening. The driver threw her one appealing glance as he came up to her. The wagon had a tilt; flapping curtains hid its interior.

'October!'

She spun round with a cry. The curtains at the back were parted. She saw a face and an extended hand and flew. The hand caught hers; she gripped the edge of the tailboard with her other hand and was drawn upward.

'Watch your step,' warned Robin. 'We have guests!'

And then in the half-darkness she saw the man with the red beard and his broad-faced companion. They were lying on the broken floor of the trolley, their hands strapped to one another's, back to back.

'You can sit on 'em if you like,' shouted Robin obligingly.

It was necessary to shout, for inside the wagon the sound of bombardment was intensified.

III

When Robin left his strange companion he went in search of a telegraph office. He had one shilling in his pocket, and that shilling had been stolen from the stall of a vendor of peppermint rock, and he was determined to take a short cut out of all his troubles. But the telegraph office was not easy to find without making enquiries. One good result came of his wanderings – he became acquainted with local topography. On a board attached to a shop was a sheet advertising the desirable character of building lots outside the town. To illustrate their proximity a conscienceless draughtsman had drawn a plan, and on one of the broad tree-shaded avenues (as they were in the drawing) was the inscription 'To Farnham.'

And Farnham or thereabouts was his immediate destination.

The town boasted, in addition to a cinema, a theatre. He became aware of this, oddly enough, before he had seen the lurid posters which advertised that sterling attraction 'A Mother's Sin,' which was immodestly described as 'The Most Stupendous Drama of Love and Hate and Woman's Sacrifice ever presented on the English Stage.'

It was an argument between the pugnacious driver of a lorry that had evidently transported the properties and scenery of this soul-stirring play, and one who, to judge by his commanding manner and all-round insolence, was not only the manager but the leading man of the troup, that first attracted Robin's attention.

He was not near enough, nor did he penetrate the fast-gathering crowd, to learn the cause of the dispute, but guessed that money entered into the question.

It was as he strolled off that he became dimly aware that there were more police in the town than seemed necessary. Two men, walking together in front of him, were obviously detectives. One took off his hat and showed a sandy head, bald at the back. They were talking; he got nearer to them.

'... not in ten years. Last case was when Mickey got Norey the Lawyer. Cut his throat same as this feller's was cut.'

That was all, and more than Robin wanted to hear. The body had been found, and though his own name had not been mentioned, he knew that he was the explanation for this incursion of police officers. They were looking for him, and either knew that he was in the town or guessed that this was the most likely place to find him.

Soon after this he found the telegraph office, took a form to the wall desk and considered. To send such a wire at all was repugnant to him. He was quitting. Whichever way he examined his motives, he was a quitter. But there was October to be considered ...

He dropped point of pencil to the paper; checked his hand again. What good would be the wire if they arrested him for the murder of 'O'? He got a little hot under the collar as he thought of all the possible consequences of such an arrest.

He made up his mind quickly, scribbled a note to the girl and looked round for a messenger. A boy had brought in a wire for despatch and was paying the clerk. Robin caught his eye and signalled him: the small boy came suspiciously.

'Here's a shilling for you, son: take this note to a young lady you'll find waiting outside the druggist's.'

When the messenger had gone, Robin walked without haste to the door and stepped aside to allow a newcomer to enter.

'Morning!'

Red Beard was more shocked than he; his voice trembled so slightly that an ordinary hearer would not have detected the quaver of it. Behind him was Lenny, a set grin on his face, his brown eyes saying as plainly as words, 'Too near – and too many police around.'

'Come right in, Reddy' – Robin's voice was cool, desperately polite – 'Tickled to death to see you.'

He had started at an advantage; his left hand was in his jacket. By a scarcely imperceptible flicker of eye had Red Beard observed this potent fact.

'Got kind of spruce, ain't you? Never seen you with a moo-stache before. You're a dude, 'bo, ain't he, Lenny?'

'Thasso,' grunted Lenny.

'I'll be going along,' said Robin.

Red Beard stepped aside promptly. As he came on to the street Robin turned at an angle to face them.

'Listen' – Red Beard seemed to have forgotten that he wanted to go into the office at all – 'I'd like to talk to you. Suppose you come a walk?'

'Suppose!' replied Robin sardonically. 'Where's the cemetery anyway?'

'Aw! Cemetery!' Red Beard looked pained. 'What's all this cemetery stuff? Me and Lenny will walk in front. That's fair, ain't it, Lenny?'

Lenny agreed in the usual manner.

Curiosity was one of Robin Leslie's weaknesses.

'Walk,' he said, and kept close behind them as they marched together side by side in their soldier-like way. They turned at the corner of the block, he close behind them, knowing the dangerous nature of corners. At the end of the thoroughfare was a fair sprinkling of people, a booth or two. A man, patently Eastern of origin, was selling hot edibles briskly. Farther down the street a procession was forming, and here was a bigger and younger crowd. There was a circus in town: gilded wagons, beautiful but under-attired ladies hobnobbed with gorgeous Cossacks; clowns smoking cigarettes, a dispirited lion blinking sleepily through the shutter that covered his cage; two camels (Robin observed that one was mangy), and a top-hatted huntsman with a mixed pack of performing hounds that were merely dogs; a band wagon of scarlet and gold and, a long way behind the tail of this aggregation of talent and beauty, a very ancient trolley with a bedraggled tilt.

'Let's talk.'

Red Beard and his companion stopped and came about with military exactness.

'I seen your young lady in the village,' said Red Beard. 'That's one nice girl. A perfect lady – ain't she, Lenny?'

'Thasso,' said Lenny.

'Me and Lenny's been talking about you. Lenny reckons that you're mad at us for shootin' you up at Boo-loyne. But we was all wrong. Mistook you for a tramp who put dirt on me an' Lenny down in Paris last fall. Ain't that so, Lenny?'

'Thasso,' said Lenny.

'We got you wrong, 'bo, and that's a fact. Now me an' Lenny don't want any fuss – we got our own graft an' we don't want anybody to go sour on us because we mistook you for a guy that doubled us in Paris.'

'And when,' asked Robin blandly, 'did you make this discovery? Did it coincide – '

'How's that?' asked Red Beard.

'Did it happen when you found that I'd borrowed a gun and was good enough shot to take your hat off?'

'That's nothin' to do with it,' Red Beard hastened to assure him. 'You didn't need to shoot off my derby – I'd take it off to you as a shooter. Yes, sir.'

'Then what do you want to talk about?'

Red Beard did not look at his friend. He stared straight ahead.

'You're in bad. Seen the coppers in town? I'll bet you have! I'll bet there's nothin' you don't see! Sharp! That's what I says to Lenny: "I'll bet he don't miss any!" '

'Yes, I've seen the police: I thought they were after you.'

Red Beard was amused. He laughed loud and long.

'Tha's the best one I heard since I left New York! Say, Lenny, did you hear this big stiff? Ain't he the big joke? Listen – I'm tellin' you. You got to get out of town – quick! There's three fly cops on every way out – and mounted fellers. You can't get out one-handed and that's a fact. But me an' Lenny won't leave you. We got a feelin' we'd like to pull you out with us. Only we can't take your young lady. That's a fact.'

'How are you going to get me out?'

Red Beard looked round, and it occurred to the fugitive that until that moment his would-be rescuer had not considered a method. The ramshackle trolley was drawn up by the road-side; its little driver sat with his back to a high poster-covered fence, eating.

'Just wait,' said Red Beard, and walked slowly over to the luncher.

'Mornin', boss – come far?'

The little man eyed him unfavourably over his glasses.

'Farnham,' he said briefly, and took another bite at the thick wad of brown dough that occupied his attention.

'Me and my friends reckon we'd like to go back to Farnham. Startin' soon?'

'Yes' – with a glance at 'my friends'. And then, with a shake of head: 'My old lorry don't go fast enough. You'd get there sooner by train.'

Red Beard whistled softly.

'Pretty well known around here?'

'I'd say,' said the lorry owner complacently. 'You wouldn't find nobody here that didn't know me. My name's Walkley.'

'Police know you?'

'Hey?' Suspicion in the man's face and tone. He had money in his pocket and this man was a foreigner. 'Yes. I don't suppose there's a constable in this country that don't know me.'

He wrapped the remainder of his lunch in brown paper.

'I'll be getting along,' he said.

Red Beard signed to the others to come; they were crossing the road. Mr Walkley's heart sank into his little boots.

'We figured we'd like to take a ride with you,' said Red Beard, and, as the old man went to the starting handle, signalled the two into the back of the machine.

The engine raved round; Mr Walkley leapt to his seat with great agility when he saw that his questioner had disappeared. The lorry shocked forward ... behind the driver the curtain was pulled aside.

'Drive straight through town and speak to nobody. I'll be watching you, you old hound, an' I'll blow your spine outer you if you squeal!'

The muzzle of a gun rested on the back of the driver's seat. Mr Walkley reeled. As the lorry came to the thronged avenue:

'You guys better lay flat,' said Red Beard, 'case any of these hicks peek in,' and set an example, lying athwart the floor, holding back the front curtain with one hand his gun levelled in the other.

Robin and Lenny were stretched side by side and facing. Half the width of the trolley was between them.

They were clear of the town, beyond the shacks that were qualifying for entrance to the gazetteer ... fields on either side ... no sign of October.

'Put that gun down!'

Red Beard turned his head. Robin was resting on his elbow, and his left hand held a black-barrelled automatic. Red Beard looked at Lenny and the impassive face of the echo told him nothing. He laid down the revolver very carefully, and Robin kicked it towards himself. And then, every muscle in play, he flung himself back against the side of the wagon. Lenny struck, but struck short. Swifter than eye could follow, his hand had moved ... the knife buried itself in the wooden floor and the point protruded beneath.

'Come here, Reddy, and step lively! Stay down – you!'

He was on his feet. Red Beard lurched forward, his hands above his head.

'Lie down – back to back.'

There were little straps in the lorry: the pinioning was easy.

'Clever, ain't you ... we got you out of town and this is what you do! Say, we'll get you for this!'

'Don't talk,' said Robin ominously.

He took a look at the driver. The little man was as if in a trance.

'Go right on: don't stop till you get to Farnham.'

Now he saw the slim figure by the wayside and, going to the back curtain, called ...

IV

As they cleared the first cross-road Robin pointed to the exit, helped her drop to the road. The lorry thundered on.

'Which way now?'

She sounded breathless, and he looked at her keenly.

'London now,' he said.

The railway had run parallel with the road for the last few miles, and they crossed it without meeting anything more human than a dog. At a wayside pond he stopped to toss into the still water a number of deadly weapons that he had acquired in the course of the trip. Two knives, a revolver and a small automatic went to their permanent rest.

'I'm rather sorry for Lenny,' he said. 'Effective knife-throwing is largely a matter of balance – it may take him years to get used to a new armoury.'

She shivered, and again he shot an anxious glance at her.

'You're not feeling – sick?' And, when she shook her head: 'You'll never deceive me about that, will you?'

'No – I'm not sick. Not *really* sick. I'm just – I'm frightened to confess it – but my nerves are – well, you can guess.'

'You have seen the newspapers?' he asked quickly.

'No; – why? Is it about the tramp? Did they find the – the body?'

He nodded.

'I haven't seen them, but I gathered from such talk as I overheard that O's body was found and that the old man had not been heard of. Of course they blame me – the garage man spilt the beans. I am aching to see the newspapers.'

He saw them much sooner than he expected.

They reached the inevitable London Road and turned eastward.

'They will shout like blazes as soon as I am out of earshot, and the funny little man will stop his machine and untie them – unless he has the sense to drive them to the nearest police station.'

He laughed at the memory of a good joke.

'What is it?' She was inclined to be irritable.

For answer he put his hand in his pocket and drew out a respectable handful of Treasury notes.

'Nearly a hundred pounds – I took every penny they had,' he said simply.

October was past surprise.

'I don't understand – anything,' she said. 'Why did you – rob them? Surely they were trying to help you? If it had not been for them you would still have been in town – captured probably.'

He was tickled at this.

'The Managing Director wouldn't allow that! I told you she wouldn't. And of course she was there – I saw the car as I was talking to Reddy at the telegraph office. No, she would hate to see me pinched – hullo!'

She had left his side and, walking to a grassy bank at the side of the road, sat down. Her face had gone suddenly very white, her hands were trembling.

'I don't think I can walk any more,' she said unsteadily.

In a state of panic Robin made a search of the road. It was a straight, broad avenue, and he thought he saw the white gable of a house through the trees.

'You won't faint if I leave you?' She shook her head. 'Sure?'

'Don't be silly – I shan't faint. Hunger doesn't kill the first day!'

Hunger! She had eaten nothing since seven that morning. He searched his pockets frantically.

'What a callous brute I've been!' he exclaimed. 'I've nothing – not even a crust.'

Without another word he sprinted down the road. As he came nearer to the gable he saw it was a house of some size. An old-fashioned place, white and chaste, its walls hidden for half their height by some creeping flower of brilliant purple. As he pushed open the gate he was staggered to see, on a neatly-painted board nailed to a big sycamore, 'Rooms to Let.'

He rang the bell, and after a wait of a minute the door was opened by a melancholy-featured maid in black. He supposed her the maid from the white apron and cap she wore. He thought she was between forty and fifty. She had been weeping; her eyes were very red and swollen, her nose had been streaked with powder hurriedly, in a pathetic endeavour to hide the evidence of her distress.

'May I see your mistress, please?'

Her eyes winked rapidly.

'Can I have a room – two rooms? My – er, my wife has been taken ill on the road.'

She shook her head half-heartedly, measured his inches with a glance.

'Would you be staying long?' she asked.

'I don't know; everything depends.'

He could almost watch the process of vacillation.

'Come in, please.'

She closed the door behind him. He was in a large vestibule from which a staircase wound up to a gallery that ran all four sides of the hall. Facing him on the wall was a large steel engraving of Queen Victoria. The floor was paved in squares of black and white tiling; there was a bloated rosewood cabinet against one wall, and an old grandfather's clock ticked solemnly in one corner. She opened a door and showed him into a parlour that was a type of all that mid-Victorian parlours should be. Everything was specklessly clean, but terribly worn and shabby. The original design of the carpet had long since disappeared: it was a reddish-blue smudge.

She took off her apron and cap and laid them on the horsehair couch.

'I am the lady of the house,' she said simply. 'I have only one maid. I – I sometimes open the door to strangers. You wanted rooms?'

'Two,' he said, but she shook her head.

'I have one – a large double room. You see, Mr ... ?'

'Robin.'

' – Mr Robin, I have no boarders any longer. I am rather far from London and not exactly in the best part of Hampshire, and in the past few years new boarding-houses have been opened. Sometimes in the spring and autumn I have a family from Southampton.'

She wanted to tell him something, but he, growing impatient as he thought of October, was in no mood for her confidences.

'May I bring her, then?' he asked.

She hesitated again.

'Yes, please. I am sure that I am doing right. God has performed great miracles for me – I must trust you.'

With this cryptic utterance in his ears but hardly in his mind, he raced back to where he had left October, and a load rolled off his heart when he saw her walking slowly towards him.

'You angel! I thought you would at least need carrying!'

She smiled at this, and October seldom smiled.

'What have you unearthed?' she asked. 'Robin, I could eat grass.'

He told her of his new landlady.

'Poor soul – how brave!' said October in a hushed voice. 'And I love early Victorian furniture, especially tables with chicken salad and apple pies and melons ... ugh! I mustn't think of it!'

She was waiting at the door and informed them quaintly that she was usually called 'Miss Ellen.'

'There is only one thing I would ask of you,' she said, after she had ceremoniously introduced the drawing-room to October, 'and that is to make as little noise as possible. I – I have an invalid in the house. My – my dear father.'

She searched rapidly for her handkerchief. Here, then, was the source of tears.

'Perhaps you would like dinner? It is rather late – we dine at midday, but if you wish – ?'

October wished, most fervently. Miss Ellen glided from the room and closed the door softly upon them.

'In many ways,' said Robin, glooming down on the girl, 'this isn't Real! It is one of the Things that Cannot Be. Thank God for money!'

He rustled the notes in his pocket luxuriously and then:

'In a moment of temporary insanity, I said – er – I wanted a room for – don't faint! – my wife and myself. There is only one room,' he said, with elaborate indifference. 'I mean bedroom. I will break it to our dear lady that I have an eccentric desire to sleep on the Chesterfield – maybe there is a davenport somewhere. To a man who has spent a very considerable time sleeping on hard ground and regarding coal sheds and French hayricks as sybaritic, a sofa, or even a reasonably soft carpet, will be heaven.'

She said nothing in reply; for some reason or other the moment was embarrassing.

'I suppose – I *am* married?' she asked.

He was astonished.

'If you don't know, who does?'

She looked hard at the window.

'I will tell you about it some time or other – I have my doubts. At any rate, I was married in circumstances that make it pretty certain it can be dissolved. Even if Mr Loamer does not take steps.'

He staggered at this.

'Mr Loamer – you're not really married to ... good heavens!'

'Why – I thought you knew?'

He shook his head.

'I knew that you were married to somebody – if I hadn't been a little mad I would have sent you back to your husband. This is the first chance I have had of talking to you – tell me all about it.'

'Confidence for confidence,' she challenged. 'Why are you a tramp?'

He scratched his chin at this and looked past her.

'Because I am a fool, I think – in fact, I know. October, do you ever bet?'

She shook her head.

'Then don't! I have been betting all my life, not only on horses and markets – they're fairly innocuous, but on whether I could stand on my hands for ten minutes without dying of apoplexy, and fool things like that. I once walked across America, from New York to Sacramento. I won ten thousand dollars and lost the best part of half a million. But a fresh sophomore – that's a second-year man at Harvard – bet me I couldn't do it, and I went after his money. Hiking isn't any effort to me; it is my chief pleasure in life.'

She nodded.

"You're walking for a bet?'

'In general,' he answered cautiously. 'In particular, I am walking for my life.'

She told him the story of her own experience, and he listened incredulously.

'It doesn't sound real. Loamer, eh?' He whistled. 'Of course you're not married! I'll bet the Managing Director thought this out!'

'The Managing Director? Oh, you mean his mother? You have met her?'

He nodded.

'A great old lady.' He chuckled at the recollection. 'She's crazy about romantic propositions. I dined with them one night, the night before I left civilisation, and she tried so hard to get me interested in a scheme for extracting electricity from thunder-clouds – it's a fact. A million pounds' capital was the modest sum required, and she was so plausible I nearly fell for it! She's the Managing Director all right. I honestly believe that Loamer hasn't a word to say in any of the dinky little transactions that have brought him into the gutter.'

She was grave at this.

'He is ruined, then?'

He nodded.

'Doubly ruined, if I succeed in walking into his office and claiming my stake. Trebly ruined – if I don't.'

And then the full understanding of the danger swept over her and left her white and shaking.

'I see now,' she breathed. 'He trapped you into making this wager. You became a tramp from the moment it was made – an unknown man, without an identity. And if you were found dead one morning, nobody would imagine that you were – oh, how horrible!'

'Ingenious,' he murmured.

And then, to his amazement, she turned on him in a fury.

'Why don't you take the first train back to town? Why do you persist in this stupid adventure? Telephone now for the police – '

She was halfway to the hall when he caught her by the arm and drew her back gently.

'I want to get out of this without explanations,' he said quietly. 'Naturally. I am not anxious to stand before the world revealed as a first-class fool. If I send for the police now, there is a murder to be explained, and publicity which I am anxious to avoid. I've got to get back to London, October, in a quiet and normal way, recover my identity, settle with Mr Loamer on the best terms I can – I don't even think I shall kick him – and when that is done we will turn our attention to your sad case. If you are married, we'll find a way of annulling the marriage – but I don't for one moment imagine you are.'

She raised her face with a jerk.

'Would you be … terribly relieved if my marriage were dissolved? That is, if it needs dissolving.'

He looked at her queerly.

'I guess *you'll* be relieved, you poor little hobo-ess!'

'You're evading!' she accused.

He eyed her steadily.

'If this marriage is dissolved, will you marry me?' he asked, and her hand shot out to him and was imprisoned.

Miss Ellen knocked at the door. 'Dinner is ready,' she said. She hoped they would excuse her shortcomings and (this was asked as Robin was following into the dining-room) when might she expect the baggage.

He turned back and produced his money. It would, he explained, take some time to get his baggage. He was only staying because his wife was not well. As a matter of fact they were on a visit from Canada and they had brought no baggage at all. He intended (a very bright notion) to ask her whether she would be so kind as to buy a few things for his wife in town – possibly a few articles for himself? A ready-made suit, for example? He had a roll of notes in his hand as he spoke. Would she accept a week's board in advance? He could have sworn that her eyes lit up at the suggestion.

By the time he joined October at the table she was half-way through the first course. Miss Ellen herself waited on them. She had, she said in some confusion, a very good wine.

'The cellar has not been touched since dear father – went away,' she said. 'He has been a traveller and has only just returned.'

The wine was pleasant enough. She gave them the history of its laying down – the name of the merchant who had supplied it in the late days of the war. The coffee, on the other hand, was thin and unpalatable.

'Of course she's English!' scoffed Robin when the girl expressed her doubt. 'Taste the coffee and be convinced!'

Miss Ellen came in soon after; she was dressed for the street and, to his delight, expressed her willingness to buy whatever he required. Perhaps they would inspect their room after her return? If not, it was the door facing them when they reached the head of the stairs.

'Mrs – er – Robin will see her room when you return,' said Robin emphatically.

He made a hurried list of his requirements and handed pencil and paper to October, walking discreetly to the window whilst she described her more intimate needs.

The dining-room overlooked a broad lawn flanked by flower-beds blazing with early chrysanthemums. There was a little wooden nesting-place on the end of a pole, weatherworn cupids at odd corners. Beyond the lawn a 'carre' of trees, as they call these narrow plantations in Norfolk; beyond that, to his surprise, a railway. It seemed to skirt the end of a kitchen garden, sketchily revealed through the plantation.

After Miss Ellen's departure, October went up to inspect her room and he found his way into the grounds. The lawn was delightfully soft; the gravelled path led to a pergola unseen from the window. Dorothy Perkins still bloomed pinkly, but there was a suggestion of neglect here.

'Poor soul!' October had said rightly. He sensed a hard and bitter fight against the encroachment of poverty, an heroic, vain defence in face of overwhelming odds. It is hard to keep the wolf from the cottage door with its one entrance – here were so many approaches to guard.

The belt of pines cut off the track garden; a low hedge, which was neither box nor privet, separated this land from a broad meadow. A small cowshed in one corner was closed. A train thundered past; he walked to the untrimmed bushes that were the first boundary-line.

Untrimmed, broken ... why broken? There was a distinct gap ... newly broken. The twigs that were snapped showed whitely, except in one place. A dark red turning brown. Blood! There it was again on the burnished face of a leaf ... and on another broken twig. He looked down. The grass grew high here, there was an abundance of dandelion ... a patch was crushed down, their stems snapped ... blood on the golden flower, too!

And now he began to quarter the field; found nothing until he explored the plantation. Under a tree very close to the path through which he had walked was a grimy old gold cap, and when he picked it up it was damp ... blood! He wiped his hand on the grass and dropped the cap where he had found it. He looked at the house. It had a brooding air: the very windows seemed to leer slyly as though enjoying some grim jokes at his expense.

'Nerves!' said Robin, and returned to the house very thoughtful.

V

October was in the drawing-room reading a newspaper with an expression more serious than his own.

'I found this under the pillow of the sofa,' she said, and gave it to him.

There was a heavy-type line across the front page.

POLICE RESERVES OF HAMPSHIRE
SEARCHING FOR TRAMP MURDERER.

'That is good to begin with,' he said, after he had read the line aloud.

'There's worse to come,' she said; but he was reading the 'worse.'

> The alleged abductor of Mrs Loamer cuts the throat of a fellow tramp and burns the building to hide his fiendish crime.

'They called me "fiendish" before,' he complained.

'Have you read what the garage man has to say?' she asked.

He jumped the headlines and came to Al Luke, his story.

> It was round about seven when I saw the tramp. He stopped at Mr Stone's garage, where I work, and asked me for a tin of petrol. I saw his hands were stained, but little dreamt that the sanguinary fluid –

'I'll bet Al didn't say that,' protested Robin.

> – sanguinary fluid was the blood of his wretched victim. I saw Mrs Loamer. She sat in the machine most of the time. She looked pale and wan. I would not call her pretty, but she was sad looking –

'He wouldn't call you pretty,' emphasised Robin.

'He doesn't even call you pretty,' she retorted.

> The man was a debased-looking creature and the trace of his vicious life was only too evident. I didn't notice what clothes he wore –

'Good for him!'

> I only saw his besotted face. Madness glared out of his eyes …

The report concluded with the information that the witness was expecting to get married at an early date to the prettiest girl in the village, and was moving to Aldershot to join the thriving garage company of Slitt and Silbermann as chief engineer.

'Not so bad,' said Robin, and folded up the paper. 'I wonder what happened to Baldy – that pathetic old slave! The paper makes no mention of him.'

At her suggestion he replaced the journal where she had found it. He left her with an old volume of Scott – the lightest reading that the bookshelf in the parlour had to offer and, returning to the garden, began a systematic search.

Nearing the end of the tree belt, he was conscious of the pungent odour of burning paraffin. Against the brick wall was a heap of ashes that still smouldered. He sniffed and raked over the ashes. The centre of the heap was still red. What had been burnt here? It was impossible to tell: the fluffy ash gave no clue, until he saw, in the depth of the red glowing heart, a hot metal button, and then another a little larger. Old clothing – and Miss Ellen did not seem the kind of woman who would burn old clothes.

Going down into the meadow, he straddled the gap in the hedge and found himself on a railway embankment. There were bloodstains here, and a heap of gravel piled up by the side of the track was scattered as though it had been struck by a heavy body.

There had been an accident. He began to piece together the evidence. Miss Ellen's aged father had wandered on to the track and had been knocked over by an engine and carried into the house. But why the mystery, and how came it that she made no reference to the happening?

Going back through the trees, he found the cap. It was an ancient golf cap with a large red check, and he had the impression that he had seen it before. But where? There must be thousands of such caps in use. He picked it up with a stick and, balancing the thing carefully, carried it to the ash heap and poked it into the centre of the fire.

When he returned to the parlour October was asleep, the open book in her lap. He sat down opposite her.

She was pretty, very pretty. The long lashes that lay on her cheek were darker than her hair, a mop of red gold ... he sighed deeply, and the sound may have awakened her, for she opened her eyes.

'Was I asleep? How long have you been here ... did I snore? How mean of you!'

He shook his head solemnly.

'Never a snore! I could have set you back a nice pair of reindeer gloves, but I didn't.'

'Why didn't you?' she asked, retrieving the book that had fallen to the floor.

'My innate delicacy is largely responsible,' he said, 'plus the dread of telling the truth when I am cross-examined in Court No VII.'

'When I am divorced?' She yawned and stretched her arms. 'Heavens – I am almost looking foward to it!'

'That almost sounds indelicate,' he replied. 'October, *quo vadis?*'

'London,' she said lazily, 'and you shall find me a nice lawyer so that I may be separated from Mr Loamer – materially and spiritually.'

He laughed gently.

' "Spiritually" is rather good! Poor old George! If it were as easy to get rid of mother as it is to get rid of wives, he'd be a happy man. October, you're unique!'

'All women are,' she retorted.

'Yes – don't interrupt: you send all my profound judgments skew-whiff! But you're unique in the light of experience. You may represent a numerous *genre*, but I have never met a sample. Vividly wholesome – "vividly" is right – you shine! Puritanical, too. That's queer. I thought you were Joan of Arc-ish, but you're not. You see no – apparitions (poor old Baldy!); you're sane. Lady Godiva is nearer the type: a shingled Lady Godiva. You would have scorned the compromise of long hair – '

She nodded.

'That is so: I should have felt I was a cheat – what else?'

'You're emotional in a kind of way – I haven't quite got to the end of you there. You're rather a stranger ... I talked blithely about winning a pair of gloves just now. But the truth is I never thought of kissing you. I'd sooner knock out the fuse of a dud shell with a coke-hammer. You'd explode – or you wouldn't. I'd be disappointed if you didn't and be unconscious if you did. How old are you?'

'Twenty-one. If I hadn't been twenty-one yesterday or whenever it was, you'd be going on your way and I should have been picking flowers for the drawing-room at Market Chase. I wonder if I should have exploded?'

'I think you would,' he nodded. 'It would have been a pretty bad piece of timing on my part. I know a fellow who jumped into the sea to save a drowning girl. She was awfully pretty and rather fond of him, but as he swam with her he kissed her – she never forgave him.'

She had not taken her eyes from his face all the time he had been speaking.

'I hate your moustache,' she said.

'That was another reason why I could not kiss you,' he said, and she went pink.

'I wasn't thinking of that – yes, I was! It is too late to start lying. I was. That moustache with little spiky ends ... like an Italian banker or Matilda Ann's ideal – '

'Hi, "O"! Can't we go by train, O? This walking is killing me.'

A cracked, choky voice hailed them, and Robin leapt to his feet.

Standing in the doorway was a little man wrapped in a woman's faded kimono. His head was swathed in white bandages, his scrawny feet were bare. Chalk-faced, he glared at Robin.

'... terribly fatiguing. You must be reasonable, O – I haven't walked so far for years ... '

It was Baldy the Tramp, Baldy tottering into this quiet parlour, the light of madness in his eyes. The old man's knees gave way as Robin reached and caught him.

'Hey?' He looked up into Robin's face. 'Hullo – I rather think the guard didn't like me to ride on the train without a ticket ... he was rather offensive ... so I got out ... I think the train must have been moving ... '

His head drooped.

'What does he say?' asked the bewildered girl. 'I can't understand.'

'He was stealing a ride on a train and the guard found him; he must have tried to escape and fallen out!'

The mystery of the bloodstains and the gap in the hedge was a mystery no longer. And the miracle of Miss Ellen's – was it not miraculous that this old wanderer should have been dropped at the door of the house he had left ten years before!

He laid the old man down on the hard sofa. His eyes were closed, and October, in alarm, thought he was dead.

'I wonder where the servant is?' asked Robin. 'Would you look after him whilst I find her?'

At that moment Baldy's eyelids flickered and opened. He looked up at Robin and smiled faintly.

'I am so dreadfully sorry to give you so much trouble, sir. My knowledge of medicine tells me that I have – um – a very short time to live. Would it be trespassing on your kindness to ask you ... I would like to see my daughter very much. I have a very big deal under way ... Mr Loamer – Loamer is arranging everything ... I am going down in the country with him to-night ... '

Across the frail body Robin's eyes met the girl's.

'Loamer! What a gentleman!' he breathed.

VI

Mr George Loamer had all his life occupied a position not easily distinguishable from bondage. The rule of that hawk-like mother of his had been a very real one, more exacting than any that the most jealous wife could have imposed.

He came back after a fruitless search for his agents to hear from the landlord of the little hotel at Alton, where she was staying, a tale and a plaint which was by now familiar.

'Madame wants me to knock two bedrooms into one, and that I can't do. I've sent to London for the caviare – there's no call for that in a little hotel like this, Mr Loamer. I'll do anything I possibly can for Mrs Loamer, but I can't perform miracles. Elwood, the florist, has sent in a bill for twelve pounds – is that all right?'

George Loamer groaned.

'Yes, that's all right,' he said miserably, and went upstairs to meet his mother.

She sat in the corner of a large new settee (purchased that day for her comfort), and she was smoking a thin brown cigarette. She looked up under her eyebrows as he came in, and flicked the cigarette into the fireplace.

'Well what has happened?'

'I can't find them anywhere,' he said miserably.

She looked at him for a long time before she spoke.

'The best surgeon in the world could not perform an operation if he had blunt instruments,' she said deliberately. 'I am disappointed in you – not for the first time.'

'But – ' he began.

She silenced him with a gesture.

'I have been sitting here reviewing the past.' She had a style which was at once pedantic and a little artificial. 'I can see no flaw in any of the schemes which my genius evolved. Failure has been entirely due to clumsy agency.'

He sat down on an inadequate chair, his hands thrust into his pockets, his big chin resting on his cravat. The very injustice of her strictures did not arouse him. The wasted nightmare years that had gone! If he could only recall any one of them, preferably the last! His blind obedience to the will of a woman who was half mad had led him from ruin to ruin, from crime to crime. And now he was involved, hopelessly involved, in the most tragic failure of all.

' ... in every detail, George! I have left nothing to chance. If you had carried out my wishes – I will not say orders – you would have been an extremely rich man by now. Do you realise that?'

He made no answer, and her further reproaches were silenced by a knock at the door. Mr Loamer started, and opened the door. It was the landlord.

'Will you step downstairs, sir?' The proprietor's voice was urgent; he was a little fearful.

'What is it?' asked Mr Loamer.

'There's a gentleman wants to see you.'

'To see me? But I know nobody here – '

Nevertheless he followed the landlord down the stairs.

There were two men waiting in the passage, tall, military-looking men, who were apparently absorbed in the study of a road map that hung on the wall of the lobby. George Loamer thought he recognised one of them. He at any rate, was recognised, for, as he came into the vestibule, the elder of the two offered his hand.

'Mr Loamer, isn't it? My name's Simpson, Central Inspector Simpson, of Scotland Yard.'

Mr Loamer felt himself change colour.

'Er – yes, I remember you, Inspector. Ten years ago, over a letter theft.'

George Loamer's knees gave under him as he followed the detective into the village street.

'There are one or two things I wish to speak to you about, Mr Loamer. I see by *The Times* that you have been recently married.'

Loamer nodded.

'And your wife has disappeared – there was an account in a local newspaper. Has she been traced?'

'Not yet,' said Mr Loamer huskily.

'When were you married?'

The big man swallowed something.

'Two days ago.'

'At – er – what church?'

'We were married by special licence – it was not in a church ... a friend of mind performed the ceremony.'

The detective was looking at him keenly.

'We shall be able to get your friend's account of that, Mr Loamer,' he said drily. 'In the meantime, there are some little matters which require elucidation, and these are the subject of my enquiry. About three weeks ago, two American gunmen arrived in this country. We have had an enquiry from the New York police; we find that they are in your employ – a man named Byrne and an Italian who is known as Lenny or Leonardo. The story in New York is that they came at your request.'

Loamer cleared his throat.

'They are in England, I know. To tell you the truth, Inspector, I met these men when I was in Chicago, and they told me that they wanted to make a new start. It was an act of philanthropy on my part to bring them to England.'

Again the detective looked at him searchingly.

'These two men are desperate characters – the most conscienceless gunmen in Chicago. What induced you to cable them five thousand dollars, with the request that they should come to England immediately?'

Mr Loamer did not answer.

'There is another enquiry from New York, and that is the more important of the two,' said Simpson. 'Little more than a month ago there arrived in this country Mr Nigel Robin Black, a very rich young American. Before leaving New York he drew from the Federal Bank a million dollars in bills – '

'As a matter of fact, he's a client of mine,' said Mr Loamer easily. 'He came to my office and asked me to undertake a rubber deal. There is no secret about that. You will find the record in my private ledger.'

'Did he place in your care the million dollars?'

Only for a second did Loamer hesitate.

'Yes,' he said. 'The money is, or was, in my bank. I have undertaken the operation he suggested – '

'Where is Nigel Black now?'

Loamer shrugged his shoulders.

'As to that I can give you no information. He is a young man full of what I might call the joy of life, and he spoke to me of taking a trip to Constantinople. I have not heard from him since.'

'Or of him?' asked the other significantly.

'Or of him,' said the desperate man. 'Why should I?'

Inspector Simpson smiled.

'It is not unreasonable to suppose that a man who trusts you with a million dollars will make a few enquiries from time to time as to its well-being. Mr Nigel Black,' he went on deliberately, 'was fond of what they call in America "hikes". In other words, he was something of a tramp. He wrote a book on the subject.'

'I was not aware of it,' said Mr Loamer.

'There is a possibility, of course,' Simpson continued, 'that Black is engaging in some fool expedition of the kind – we have in fact heard that a mysterious English tramp was seen a fortnight ago in the region of Paris. If this is he, there will be no further enquiries.'

'Enquiries?' repeated Mr Loamer, and Simpson nodded.

'The Metropolitan Police do not like men to disappear, especially rich men, Mr Loamer,' he said quietly. 'A few years ago a Dr Marcus Elvington vanished from the face of the earth, after entrusting you with his affairs.'

'It was I who notified the police,' said Mr Loamer quickly, and Simpson smiled.

'That was wise of you,' he said; 'for if you had not notified the police, somebody else would have done so. Whoever brought the matter to our attention, Dr Marcus Elvington disappeared, and has not been seen since. With him disappeared a hundred thousand pounds. There are other circumstances of your life, Mr Loamer, that are curious, but I am not prepared to discuss them at the moment.'

By now Loamer had recovered something of his old self-possession.

'Your suggestions and innuendoes are a little unusual, aren't they, Inspector?' he said. 'You seem to forget that I am a man of some position in the City of London – '

Simpson interrupted him with a gesture.

'Let us be frank with one another. It is easier, because we are not speaking in the presence of witnesses. Your house has been shaky as long as I can remember; you have speculated in all sorts of crazy adventures; you were until a few weeks ago, heavily overdrawn at your bank; and you owed an immense sum of money to one of your brother brokers. We have discovered that these debts have been liquidated, and presumed, on seeing the announcement of your marriage, that your wife's fortune had helped in this respect. I will be perfectly open with you, Mr Loamer: unless Nigel Black appears within a week, the enquiries we are making will take a more unpleasant form.' He drew on his gloves. 'I think that is about all, except that I should like you to ask Byrne and his friend to report to Scotland Yard the moment you get into touch with them.'

George Loamer went back to his mother's room, a broken man.

Mrs Loamer reclined at her ease in a long cane chair, a cigarette between her heavily carmined lips, her bright eyes fixed upon her son. That terrified man was silent; he had less reason for speech because of his mother's awful calm. A dozen times he tried to tell her of his danger – but in her presence lacked the courage to speak. He sat, numbed and silent; his fingers beat a miserable tattoo on the arm of the chair, and his mechanical smile was little more than a grimace.

It was an hour before he dared reveal the extent of their ruin. She listened without comment, but he saw the fury in her eyes and quailed beneath her unspoken scorn.

'What are you going to do?' she asked. When Mrs Loamer was annoyed, her voice had a peculiar hoarseness. And she was hoarse now.

'I don't know.' He examined the carpet attentively. 'I suppose I'd better take the car and find these two men. We must get them out of the country at once. Really, Mother, I don't see why you should blame me. I've done my best. I never supposed that Black would be easy. I told you so – '

'Never mind what you told me!' she rasped.

'At any rate,' he interrupted, 'it was not my idea: You will admit that. It was yours.'

He wilted under the contempt in her eyes.

'Not your idea! Have you ever had an idea, George? Not your idea! I hate to remind you, but you are very like your father.'

Evidently this was her deadliest insult, for there followed a long and tense silence. Mr George Loamer's face was very red; his frown was terrible; but she knew him for the weakling he was, and his active rebellion came in the nature of a shock.

'I don't care ... !' He spoke rapidly, his sentences were a little disjointed. 'I'm finished with the business. It's too horrible! And he knows ... he's always known! It was fate that he should meet October ... fate. Everything is working against us – everything. Mad! We're all mad – such a clumsy scheme. I wonder I could have listened to you. You've made things impossible. I'm going to Southampton to-morrow morning, and I'm catching the first boat that sails for New York.'

The thin lips of the woman curved in a smile.

'You sail – as a steward?' she asked sardonically. 'How will you reach New York? And what will happen when Black gets back there? "Mad," I think you said? You'll stay here, George, until I give you leave to go – and money to go with. I should have stayed in London! I never intended coming to the country. In London my mind expands – no general should overlook a battlefield. I came here because I knew that sooner or later you would need help. Have you ever succeeded in anything – without help?'

He wriggled in his impotent rage and became his old humble self.

'Mother, be reasonable! This thing is getting on my nerves; I shall have a breakdown. I get no sleep ... really, the thing is impossible. And he knows! Why not chuck the thing and go to Canada with me?'

She got up from her chair, walked to the window and pulled aside the blind; he thought she had heard something which had attracted her attention, but apparently she needed this stimulus of movement and light – stimulus or sedative, for, when she turned round, she was smiling.

'We'll go to London,' she said. 'The opera opens to-morrow and I've asked some people to my box.'

He could only wave impotent hands and utter sounds which could not be interpreted. And then:

'What is the name of that man with the red beard?'

'Byrne,' he replied, in surprise.

She nodded.

'I want to see him,' she said. 'No, not here. It would be foolish to bring them here. Where are they waiting?'

He told her that they had last telephoned from a garage on the outskirts of Farnham.

'That means, of course, that they are too well known to go into the town,' she nodded. 'And it would be little better for them here, if what you say is true.'

He was a picture of apprehension.

'Is it wise?' he pleaded. 'I mean to say ... need you come into this at all?'

'Don't be a fool!' She cut him short. 'Now tell me, what have you said to these men? What reason have you given?'

'I've told them ... that Black was a servant who has been blackmailing the family for years. That's right, isn't it? That he unearthed some ... well, some scandal about ... us.'

'Did you convince them?'

'I suppose I did' – he was doubtful. 'But they're a pretty tough crowd. Byrne wanted to know how long Black had been a hobo – as he calls him. Fortunately I wasn't obliged to go into details. One of them – the little Italian or Spaniard or whatever he is – met Robin two years ago in a hobo camp on the Frazer River in Vancouver. They called him "The Guy who Walks," because he never jumps trains – that means "steals rides." Apparently a walking tramp is an object of derision.

This Lenny man was on the run for some crime he'd committed in Chicago at the time, and apparently he had some sort of fight with Black and got the worst of it. Byrne told me that he only found this out after he'd arranged with Lenny to join him, and if it had not been for Lenny's surprise at finding an old enemy they would have got him at Boulogne.'

Another pause.

'Mother, when ... if ... '

He stopped.

'When – if?' she repeated impatiently.

'Suppose the thing goes through, what about these two men? We're rather in their hands, aren't we?'

Her frosty smile answered him.

'One of them will be killed – at least one,' she said. 'I think I know Nigel Black! Ring the bell, George, and ask the landlord to make a *coupe Jacques*.'

VII

The sound of a door opening sent Robin into the hall. It was Miss Ellen, laden with parcels, and she gave him a friendly nod – then saw his face.

'Has anything happened?' she asked fearfully.

He tried to reassure her, but, dropping the packages she carried, she ran past him into the parlour, and when he went in she was kneeling by the sofa, her arm about the old man's neck.

'Well! That is why you came, to find him, I suppose?'

She was strident, defiant; he marvelled at the valour of this frail little woman. 'I should have known that you were detectives ... that is why you sent me on this errand, so that you could spy on a poor old man.'

Hate shone in her eyes like a fire. He was too dumbfounded to answer.

'You'll have to prove that – that he killed anybody. He couldn't do it – he couldn't! And the girl – an old man like he is ... lies, newspaper lies!'

A light dawned upon Nigel Robin Black. Now he knew why the old man's bloodstained clothes had been burnt – why the newspaper was so carefully hidden from sight. This loyal daughter of his had confused her father – with Robin! He could have chuckled, and did indeed smile.

'We are no detectives,' he said quietly; 'we are tramps!'

'Tramps ... ?' Doubt and incredulity in tone and look.

'Yes: one half the newspaper story applies to me – the other half to your father.'

'You are a tramp ... which half? Which half?' tremulously. 'He didn't ... he didn't hurt ... kill anybody?'

'Let us get your father up to bed.' Robin was peremptory, almost bullying. 'We can talk about things after.'

The old man had been a silent listener, and now, as the other stooped to lift him, he tittered foolishly.

'Professor of anatomy, hey? His own knife, too! He got his! Third cervical vertebra ... '

Robin carried him rapidly out of earshot. On the bottom step of the stairs stood an old woman, wringing her hands. She was the oldest woman he had ever seen.

'Oh dear, oh lor', Miss Ellen! I only went down to boil the kettle, Miss Ellen ... '

Miss Ellen, practical in that testing time of nerves and judgment, waved her aside and flew upstairs ahead of Robin and his burden. She showed the way to a little room at the far end of the gallery.

'Thank you – I can attend to him now.'

She was as pale as the old man and almost pushed Robin from the room.

'This,' he said, as he came back to the parlour, 'is emphatically one of the Things that Cannot Be. It is impossible and absurd – the most monstrous of all coincidences that ever disturbed the smooth flow of logic's placid stream.'

'It was the old man – Baldy, as you called him?'

'Baldy; and this is his home – the home from which Loamer

enticed him. I'm only guessing now. October, we may have to move quickly.'

'Why? Do you think she will send for the police?'

He nodded.

'There is a chance. You see, she cannot believe that her father would murder; she may be seized of the notion that my conviction would free her parent from blame. The homely little lioness! S-sh!' He raised a finger in warning.

There was a telephone in the hall: they heard Miss Ellen's voice, and Robin crept to the closed door and listened.

'Dr Steel? Will you come up at once, please? My father has come home, very ill. ... Yes, my father; he has been to – to America.'

A clang as the receiver was hung up. Robin had tiptoed back to the middle of the room when the door opened. Miss Ellen's face was still white, but she had recovered her old serenity. Closing the door behind her, she stopped to straighten a linen mat on one of the small tables which abounded in the room.

'Mr Robin – '

'Black – but Robin will do,' he said.

'I want you to tell me – the truth. About my father and about yourself.' Her faded eyes fell upon the girl and their infinite pathos brought October to the verge of tears. 'I am quite alone – in the world,' she said. 'There isn't a lonelier woman in all the world. And I've nobody to whom I can turn for advice or help. Will you remember this?'

Robin nodded slowly.

'I think I can explain about your father. I will tell you everything,' he said. 'I am guessing a lot, but I don't think my guesses are very wild. Do you know Mr George Loamer?'

She nodded.

'Has your father ever had business transactions with him?'

He had guessed very near to the mark, he discovered when she told him of her father's disappearance.

'He went out one day to go to London, and I never saw him again. He had been very mysterious about a great transaction in which he was engaged. I don't think he was normal. My mother had recently died, and that had upset him terribly. At that time he was a rich man; he had inherited two large properties from his aunt, and I was worried about him. I had a wire the day he left to say he would not be back for a week, that he was going to inspect some property. The week passed, and then I went up to see Mr Loamer. He told me that father had gone abroad to buy an oil concession in Roumania. From that day to this I have not seen him.'

It was as Robin had expected. Only now was he beginning to appreciate the extent of the Managing Director's amazing system. Old Dr Elvington must have been only one of many who had disappeared or died, that this mad woman might indulge herself in extravagant speculation.

He thought of October's mother, who had died so suddenly, and his heart went cold. October saw the sudden pallor that came to his face, but happily did not understand its cause.

'I should imagine, Miss Elvington,' he said gently, 'that your father was a little abnormal the day he left you – nobody knew that better than Loamer. The doctor was taken down to Four Beeches and put in the charge of the ruffian whom he eventually killed.' And, seeing her start, he nodded gravely. 'I'm afraid that is true. The man called "O" is dead. How he came to be in Loamer's service we shall probably never know. He had plenty of money; the newspaper accounts say that the police found a hundred pounds in notes in his hip pocket. Probably the custody of your father was not the only service he rendered to Loamer.'

Miss Ellen, sitting stiffly on the edge of a chair, her hands folded in her lap, pale blue eyes searching his face, listened without interruption until he had finished.

'You think there is no doubt?' She shook her own head in anticipation of his answer. 'I'm glad – I'm glad he killed him!' she said breathlessly. 'That anybody could be so wicked and cruel to an old man!' She shuddered. 'Dreadful … he drove my father insane. And he was such a gentle soul – such a dear, gentle soul!'

With an effort of will at which Robin could only marvel she controlled her quivering lips.

She described the miracle of Dr Elvington's return. She and

the old woman had been cutting vegetables in the garden when the train had rattled past, and had heard rather than seen the old man fall from the door of the carriage in which he had been concealed until a vigilant guard found him.

'We dragged him into the house. Until he opened his eyes and called me by my dear mother's name, I did not know him. And then he told me of the – the – of what he had done, and I found the blood on his poor rags and burnt them. Mr Black, what am I to do?'

'Do nothing. You have sent for the doctor? Tell him your father is asleep and you do not wish him disturbed. No doctor can help him at present. Later, when all this talk of tramps and murders has subsided, you can call him in. The point is, Miss Ellen, what would you wish us to do?'

She had no views.

'You may stay – or go whenever it is convenient,' she said. 'I will help you however I can. I was glad you came – the presence of a man in the house was welcome. What set you tramping, Mr Black?'

He shrugged his broad shoulders.

'I was born that way, I suppose,' he said.

Miss Ellen went out soon after.

'What *did* set you tramping – originally?' October was curious.

'A woman,' he said grandly, and saw her lips curl.

'Really?' She was rather cold.

'Shall I tell you – '

She shook her head; her voice was a little strained.

'I don't expect you to table your heart for my inspection.'

'You are wise,' he agreed. 'I have no romance; I have had no violent affairs. My heart is as nearly virginal as makes no difference.'

'Somebody sent you away and you went,' she insisted. 'There is no crime in that – you have no need to defend yourself. It is not my business. I don't expect you to take me into your confidence – I should loathe you if you did. She has a right to your reticence.'

He glowered at her. One needle point of his ridiculous

moustache curled downward. Under such a handicap he could not be heroic.

'There – is – no – woman – in – my – life – but – you,' he said.

She laughed politely.

'I am not concerned,' she said.

'I could *shake* you!'

'You dare! And your moustache is coming undone!'

'Is it?' He was interested enough to approach the gilt-framed mirror above the stove. 'You did that. No self-respecting moustachios could stay jaunty in the presence of a nagging fiancée.'

'I'm not nagging – and I'm not your fiancée.'

He said nothing to this; she thought she saw a shadow pass across his face.

'I *am* nagging – and I *am* your fiancée,' she added. 'I'm an unpleasant little devil, Mr Nigel Robin Black – author. I do wish we were in London!'

He caught his breath.

'That's better!' he said. 'I had the sensation of standing on a chimney-stack a mile high and watching somebody pulling it down. Yes, it was as bad as that. Mrs Loamer was the immediate lady, but I haven't tramped for love of her.'

'Who could?' she answered sympathetically.

It was strange how shaken she was; she could hardly believe that this limp being with funny squirmy sensations inside her was October Jones ... or Loamer.

'I mustn't try that again,' she said seriously.

'Try what?'

'Entertaining the gentleman with the green eyes. Yes. I was jealous.'

He took no advantage of the opening; she would have been surprised if he had. That was the wonder of it all – she could dispense with her defences, leave the portcullis raised and the drawbridge down, and the truce, unspoken, unformed, was observed. The safety of him was like a draught of wine. Sometimes it tempted her to folly. In certain moods she was for painting 'welcome' on the portcullis and laying a carpet across the bridge. Just to see ... if he would.

A knock at the front door advertised the arrival of the doctor. Followed a long conversation between Miss Ellen and the visitor. The murmur of their voices came faintly through the stout door.

'He is going upstairs,' said Robin, in surprise.

A very long time elapsed before the voices were heard again and the front door closed. Miss Ellen came in, her eyes red with weeping.

'The doctor says my father cannot possibly recover,' she said. 'I told him he had fallen from a train, and he says that at his age the shock is too violent for any hope of recovery.'

She pressed her lips tightly together, but the tears were rolling down her cheeks.

'But the doctor doesn't know,' said Robin quietly. 'He doesn't know the hard life your father has been leading.'

She shook her head.

'I bless you for that little ray of hope,' she said, 'but the doctor is right – I feel it. And his mind has gone, though he has long lucid intervals when he knows me and remembers – everything. I am too grateful to God that He sent him home, to the hearts that loved him, to resent.'

The heroine! Robin was humbled in the presence of this homely woman, prematurely aged by her sorrows. She had given up her life for this appointed end – sacrificed youth and was grateful that the wanderer might die in the home he had desolated. After she had gone:

'Do you think he will die?' October asked in a low voice.

Robin nodded.

'She thinks so. Women have an uncanny instinct for these things.'

Dusk fell. Miss Ellen came into the parlour with a lamp and drew the blinds. She was very calm, cheerful almost. Her father was sleeping, she said. At the door she lingered.

'I have put your clothes upstairs, Mr Black. If you wish to dress before supper, they are ready for you.'

Robin had forgotten all about the clothes.

'Do you mind if I go up and change?'

October did not object.

'You will go to bed at what time you wish,' said Miss Ellen.

'Yes,' said Robin thoughtfully. 'And that reminds me, Miss Ellen. Would you object very much if I used your parlour … very late? In fact, I may be writing until the early hours – '

'We may both be writing till the early hours,' October broke in.

The woman looked from one to the other.

'I see,' she said quietly, and went out.

'What *did* she see?' asked Robin, but October was immersed in her Scott and supplied no answer.

Soon after, Robin disappeared and was gone until a few minutes before supper was announced. There walked into the room a soldierly figure in yellow tussore. He was clean-shaven; the face was well moulded – there was about him that ineffable air of good breeding which may not be stated in terms of looks.

'You?' she said incredulously.

'I,' said Robin. He fingered his cheek tenderly. 'The wasp poison has ceased to cling to my sturdy jaw. Scared away, I imagine.'

She had noticed that morning that the swelling had almost disappeared. Of the black eye, the relic of which had disfigured his face on their first meeting, nothing remained but the palest shadow.

'You – come into the light. I want to look at you.'

He obeyed without embarrassment.

'Yes … ' The scrutiny did not altogether satisfy her, it seemed. 'Yes … you are different. I wonder if I like the change? I think so.'

This new aspect of him gave her the satisfaction a new toy affords to a child. She made him stand, here and there, with the light on his face and behind him: in profile …

'Yes,' she said.

'Do I get past?'

'You get past,' she said. 'But you're terribly young!'

'I shall grow out of that,' he said tritely. 'And I'm thirty something. In our set I am an aged gentleman.'

She pondered this.

'Ten years older than I – '

'Thirteen; that's unlucky. For you, I mean. What nonsense you make me talk!'

Miss Ellen had supper with them – an act of friendliness that they appreciated each for a different reason. She remarked frankly upon his improved appearance. When the coffee came in, she left them finally.

'I have opened the bureau desk if you wish to write,' she said, 'and I have put a cover and a pillow on the sofa if you don't.'

'That lady has a nice mind,' said Robin when they were alone.

He turned the conversation to a more serious channel.

'We may stay here for a day or so,' he said. 'but we must make preparations for a flit.'

'It will be ever so much easier now that you have clothes,' she suggested, but he shook his head.

'I'm not sure of that. All depends upon how far Red Beard allowed the lorry to go before he pulled up. I've been thinking since that they may not have gone far.'

'Who is Red Beard?'

He smiled. He *had* a nice smile: she was certain of this now.

'A gunman of sorts. A tramp I pigged with in Utica told me that he was a well-known high jacker who had got into some sort of trouble in Chicago – he double-crossed one of the intelligentsia in the rum-running business and Mud became his middle name. The red beard is merely a Living Down of the Past. Lenny was with him in his various enterprises. He has been on the road (as we call it at home). I met him two years ago, when I was hiking through British Columbia and we had a – well, a sort of fight. It was over a question of property. He tried to "glom" my boots when I was asleep. They are nothing very much. Some day the slow but steady law of the United States will reach for Red Beard and set him firmly in a large wooden chair, and some electrician will buy his wife a new hat on the proceeds.'

He was observing her closely.

'You're a tired woman. If you are wise you'll go and meet Miss Morpheus. I change the sex because, as I have told you before, I am innately delicate.'

The advice was welcome. October had never felt so tired in her life. How long ago since she had slept in her hard little bed at Four Beech Farm? Ages?

He talked about the road and the queer folks of a world beyond her ken. The Gobi Desert *was* tramping. He knew a strange people, famous people in their own world. Hoke, who tramped through Russia whilst the Revolution was in fiercest flame, who ambled pleasantly through Germany during the war and begged his way from one prisoners' camp to another. Lossy, the New Englander who spoke fourteen languages and could not write his own name. And Lossy had walked and begged his way from Kashmir to Bucharest. She was immensely interested, was angry with herself that she nodded. Perhaps the monotony of his voice was studied ... she woke half-way up the stairs in his arms – he delivered her on her feet at the door of her room.

A minute later he was knocking softly on the door, begging in a loud whisper for his razor.

It was no more than the truth that he had letters to write – the writing had been postponed too long. One of these was a very long letter. His pen moved with extraordinary rapidity; sheet after sheet was covered and tossed aside. Miss Ellen brought him coffee at ten o'clock, saw the quantity and was impressed.

'There is a letter-box at the end of the road,' she said, and described its location. But there would be no collection until the morning, she said.

'I'll post to-night – a letter-box is as good as a safe deposit,' he said.

Might she bring him some refreshment before he went to bed? She suggested wine, but Robin, in haste, elected for tea. She had tea, a special brand that Dr Elvington liked. It was the first time he had heard Baldy's name – the grandeur of the appellation surrounded the old man's identity with an aura of dignity. Never again did he think of the little tramp except as Dr Elvington.

By eleven o'clock the three most important letters were finished. He went in search of Miss Ellen to beg stamps, and found her in a lofty, stone-flagged kitchen, stirring some concoction that simmered on a wood fire.

'Shall I post them?' she volunteered, when the stamps had been extracted from her notecase, but he wouldn't hear of this.

It was a fine night; the sickle moon was still in the sky, and gave an eerie half light to a dark and silent world. He walked up the drive, pulled open the gate and strolled towards the letter-box. It was let in to a stone pillar that formed a corner-stone of the small estate. He dropped the letters in and walked leisurely back. Frogs were croaking by a far-away pond, a frantically hurrying bat darted down towards him, swerved and vanished. A slow goods train was making the grade somewhere south, and the harsh cough-cough of the engine was softened by distance to the gentlest of 'woofs'. A night for the road and the open country, he thought.

His hand was on the gate.

A streak of silver in the air ... a bird? He ducked in time.

The knife struck the cross-bar of the gate – he saw the second in flight and threw himself back as he jerked out his gun. The second knife missed the gate – he heard the sharp whang of it as it struck a tree. Out of the darkness on the opposite side of the road leapt a thin pencil of flame ... once, twice. The automatic spat in reply ... a shadow ran from the shadows – Robin threw his gun to his left hand and fired. The shadow stumbled and went down.

PART THREE

I

Robin was inside the gate, running. He saw the open doorway ...

'Get away from the door!' he yelled, and Miss Ellen fell out of sight.

He leapt to the top step as October reached the hall. She asked no questions. A small lamp was standing on the hall table: she made for this and blew it out as he closed the door.

'What was it?' Miss Ellen was trembling. 'Not the police?'

'No: friends of mine – that's all.' He was out of breath but was grinning savagely. 'Lenny got his knives back – probably saw me toss them in the pond and fished them out again. I should have been prepared for that. But the gun is different – a .42. Whiskers used a hammerless of a smaller calibre.'

'They didn't hurt you?'

October's hand was moving slowly up and down his sleeve and the caress set him on fire.

'No – but I hurt one of them. Lenny, I think. I hope he isn't dead: I've a soft spot for the wife of the jail electrician and I'd hate her to be robbed of her new hat. I'll make sure.'

He went through the parlour, extinguished the light and, opening a window noiselessly, dropped on to the flagged terrace beneath. Passing through the tree belt, he reached the place where the old man's clothes had been burnt. There was a weatherbeaten door in the wall and he had noticed that it was not quite closed. He pushed it open far enough to squeeze through. He was in a narrow alleyway flanked on one side by the wall of the garden and on the other by a wire fence. Along this he crept, pausing every few paces to listen. Presently he was within a few yards of the road. He calculated that he must be opposite the spot where the shadow fell ... The purr of a motor-car growing fainter and fainter. He reached the road and looked left and right.

The road was very straight; half a mile away he saw a speck of red light – the tail-lamp of a car, and as he looked, it went out of sight. The automatic was in his left hand now: he was taking no chances.

Nobody was there – not even in the black shadows of the trees in front of him. They had gone. He stepped into the middle of the road, the moonlight reflected on the polished barrel of his gun. No sound or movement. The nearest house was a quarter of a mile away, and only congenital idiots come out at night to learn the cause of promiscuous shooting. Doubtless there were timid souls at this moment 'phoning urgently to the police.

Here ... or was it here that Lenny fell? He took a chance and lit a match ... dropped it instantly as the sound of pattering feet came to his ears.

It was October. She wore an old coat over her nightdress and was barefooted.

'Get back to the house!' he hissed.

'Don't be a cave-man,' she said. 'They've gone. I saw the car drive up and somebody lifted in. I went up to my bedroom and looked out of the window. It isn't as clever as climbing the garden wall, but you see a lot more! Is this the knife?' She held a long-bladed, wicked-looking hunting knife in her hand. 'It was sticking in a tree – '

He raised his hand in warning and listened.

'That's probably a police tender,' he said, and they ran to the house and closed the door. Miss Ellen, waiting like a wilting ghost in the gloomy hall, rubbed her thin hands together nervously.

'Will they come here?' she asked, when he told her.

'They may enquire – you had best tell them that you heard the shots. October can go back to her room. I don't imagine that they will wish to search the house. If you went down to the gate that might save a lot of trouble.'

She nodded: she had nerve and to spare. So it came about that when the police arrived, and behind them a dozen or so residents in the neighbourhood, Miss Ellen was able to give the only authentic story of the shooting.

'Didn't see any of 'em, did you?' asked the police sergeant, for Miss Ellen claimed to have been a witness from *her* bedroom window. 'One a red-bearded man? He was in Farnham this afternoon?'

No, Miss Ellen had not identified a red-bearded man or any other kind of man. The police made a sweeping examination of the ground and found blood traces to confirm the lady's story.

'Wasn't a tramp – feller in a brown suit ... moustache waxed up – with a girl?'

Miss Ellen had seen no such tramp.

'That's certainly queer.' The sergeant scratched his head. 'Motor-car and all that! Didn't see that either, Miss Elvington? I'm telling everybody there's trouble coming to any tramp I find with a gun – and that's a fact!'

He went off to collect evidence from the other inhabitants. One had heard six shots fired – one had only heard two. The firing was over something under a minute: on that point they were all agreed.

And then a discovery was made by accident. The post-box at the corner of the road had been broken open and rifled. It was not a very difficult operation, for roadside boxes are not designed to resist the attention which had been paid to this.

'A gang of mail thieves,' concluded the sergeant vaguely.

At long last the patrol wagon departed town-wards, the neighbours disappeared behind doubly locked doors, and Miss Ellen went back to the dark parlour.

'They've gone! And the post-box has been broken open – '

She was shaking so that she had to sit down. But the indomitable woman's rest was short. She went upstairs – her father was still sleeping.

There were wooden shutters to the parlour window: these, as a matter of precaution, Robin closed before he lit the lamp again.

'Go along and sleep,' he said.

October shook her head vigorously.

'I couldn't. Honestly. I'll stay up till I feel tired.'

She lifted one bare foot after the other and brushed them clean of the sand.

'Then for heaven's sake dress,' he said; 'and dress warmly, because I'm going to say something to you that will make your blood run cold!'

'This,' said October, as she made for the door obediently, 'this will be an interesting night.'

She was down in a few minutes, if not wholly, at least cosily, dressed.

'Produce your creep,' she said.

He was pacing up and down the long room, his hands clasped behind him. She wondered why he frowned and whether there was really something serious to hear.

'Police car or no police car – Lenny dead or Lenny alive – those birds have not roosted for the night.'

'They will come back?'

'Yes, sir; sure as you're born!'

'When you have finished being idiomatic in the Darktown manner, will you please tell me why you think this?'

He was laughing softly.

'You've got a nerve – "Darktown manner"! I'll reduce it to good English. I'm too near the winning post – that's permissible – for Mrs Loamer to let up – relax her efforts, I mean. She's that kind. There is only one thing that will stop her and it isn't a gun – but a fountain pen!'

She shook her head, all at sea.

'Don't you understand? For the first time since – I've lost track of time – I am in a position to write – and I wrote. And they saw me post and duly reported to General Headquarters, which was, I suspect, in the car. They went after the letters and got them. Therefore do I say that the night is still young for Mrs Loamer – I wonder what her pet name was.'

'What did you write in the letters?' she asked curiously.

'There was one important and vital sentence in the most important and vital of the letters – it ran somehow like this, and was at the beginning:

> This is practically a copy of the letter I sent you from Winchester last night, but I am scared of the first going astray.

'*Did* you write from Winchester last night?' she asked in surprise, and he shook his head.

'No – it was an inspiration to start with, that passage. The only question is: will Cleopatra call my bluff?'

'Cleo – you mean Mrs Loamer? But who was the letter meant for?' she asked.

'A friend – his name is Mortimer and he is, to be exact, a domestic servant in the employ of a lunatic.'

'In other words, your valet,' she said. 'And my blood isn't running cold and I'm terribly disappointed.'

He suggested, unhelpfully, bed and a good night's sleep. She searched for her book, tidied away by Miss Ellen, and found it. Robin went back to his pen and ink and began writing letters all over again. The clock in the hall had a soft, musical chime.

Looking up from her book, October counted twelve. Robin glanced round at her.

'Is your hearing good?' he asked softly.

'Yes – why?'

He did not answer: his eyes wandered to the door.

'There is a bell ringing somewhere.'

She heard it now, a mournful clang-clang, muffled by the interposition of many doors.

'Do you think it is Miss Ellen – her father may be worse. Shall I go – ?'

He waved her down, and was half-way to the door when it flew open. It was Miss Ellen and her teeth were chattering.

'Somebody at the door – ringing!' she gasped. 'Past twelve … there is a car in front of the house … '

'Oh?' Robin's face was blank, expressionless. 'Would you like me to open?' he asked.

Miss Ellen's voice was twitching.

'No – I will open!' Her voice was strained and unnatural. 'I will open – '

She went firmly from the room; he followed her, signalling October to put out the light. In the open doorway he slipped his gun from his pocket and covered the door behind the unconscious Ellen Elvington. A rattle of chain and the creak of the lock.

'Who is there?' she asked.

'A lady who wishes to see Mr Nigel Black.'

Robin nearly let his pistol fall in his astonishment.

For the woman who spoke was Mrs Loamer!

'Ler her in!' he whispered, and stepped back into the parlour. Fortunately October had turned the lamp low.

Mrs Loamer was alone: he saw this when her tall figure was silhouetted against the open doorway.

'Come in,' he said, and stepped aside to let her pass.

In her white-gloved hands she carried a pair of lorgnettes. She raised them and favoured October with a long and steady scrutiny, and such was the girl's disposition and balance that she grew neither angry nor embarrassed under the ordeal, but gave gravity for insolence.

'Is this – the girl – my son's wife?'

'That is October – at present nobody's wife,' he answered quietly.

'Really!'

An ironical politeness can be very offensive. And yet Mrs Loamer had no desire to be offensive. She came bearing large flags of truce with an ink-wet deed of armistice ready for his signature. Literally she carried in the shagreen bag that dangled from her wrist a document which represented both armistice and lop-sided reparation.

'I should like to talk with you – alone,' she said.

Miss Ellen stood with folded hands just inside the room. She faded away at the words.

'Would you like me to go?' October needed only the agreement in his eyes to follow her hostess. Robin closed the door.

'Now,' he said, 'won't you sit down?'

The old woman declined with a gesture.

'I suppose you are going back to London?' she began conventionally.

'I hope so,' he said. He was very careful in the choice of words. 'You have read my letter?'

Her eyebrows rose.

'I do not remember that you wrote to me?'

'I didn't; I can't remember when I wrote last to you. But I gather that you *have* read my letter?'

She ignored the question: indeed, it was one not to be answered without placing herself at a great disadvantage, and just now it was necessary that she should maintain command of a very delicate situation.

'Mr Black,' she began, 'I have come to you in preference to sending my son – who is rather ... well ... '

'A mug,' he suggested.

The vulgarity pained her.

'I don't mind admitting that my son's affairs are in a hopeless state ... that will be a shock to you?'

'I should be shocked if they weren't,' he said, and he saw the anger in her eyes.

'Mr Black, we are in all sorts of trouble. Market Chase to keep up, my place in Kensington, and heavy losses in my son's business – due to his wholly ignoring my advice – we are simply ruined by – '

'Current expenses?' he suggested when she paused. 'They must be fairly heavy. I do not know what is the current rate for gunmen, but it must be heavy. Even the second-raters are expensive, I should imagine. You are feudal-minded, Mrs Loamer. I have often wondered why your ginger-bearded retainer doesn't wear your badge on his chest – two wolves couchant on a lamb rouge, isn't it? Lenny would look fine in a suit of armour carrying your flaming banner.'

She accepted his banter without visible resentment. He could admire her without reservations, having discounted her peculiar morals. Over seventy and as straight as a lance. Fascinating, too, with her wonderful eyes as black as night and as fathomless. The Roman nose had a quality of its own; less in evidence, she would have been a beautiful woman.

'You interrupted me.'

'I'm sorry!'

She laid the shagreen bag on the table where he had been writing, took out a folded slip of paper and smoothed it flat.

'I cannot help feeling that you blame my son for all the stupid things that have happened since – since the night you dined with us. That seems an awful long time ago, doesn't it? It was most unfortunate that you should have met George in New York – '

'But more unfortunate that I met him in London.'

His voice was silky; he was smiling. She shivered a little, knowing the kind of man he was. Such were deadliest when they were most cheerful. He had shaken her. She had experienced a spasm of fear and he knew it.

He had seen the slip of paper she had smoothed open on the writing table. The colour and shape were familiar. But he said nothing, waiting for her to explain a visit that now needed no explanation.

'Shall I be very frank, Mr Black?' He inclined his head. 'I want to get back to London. My agents have found a delightful villa for me at Cannes. I shall sell Market Chase and Four Beeches and leave the country. But I have a fearful number of bills to pay, and some of my creditors are getting unpleasant. I wish to start with a clean slate, and that can only be done if you will help me.'

'To what extent?'

She picked up the cheque: it was already filled in, wanted nothing but a signature. The sum was a very large one. It was indeed the sum he had already deposited with Mr George Loamer. He smiled again and handed back the paper.

'No,' he said.

He did not say that he was sorry. He was not sorry at all, and he was very honest.

'No?'

Her head hung to one side; the lips were tightened.

'It means an awful lot of bother – for both of us. I should hate to see you in one of our English courts and the whole ghastly business exposed. Naturally, being what you are, it is unlikely that you would allow yourself to be arrested for murder without a fight. It would be perfectly horrible to hear that you had been shot down like a dog by some wretched policeman – '

'Or gunman,' he suggested. 'Such accidents happen in a free-for-all fight and the murderer has the support of a righteous act. I'm sorry – I interrupted you.'

'That I wish to avoid. I would like to see you ride in comfort to London, without fuss or scandal. I suppose this girl means nothing to you?'

She watched him keenly and would have been happy to have found a new and more effective lever.

'We will not discuss "this girl",' he said.

One shoulder went up – he knew the sign; could have foretold her next words.

'Well ... there is nothing to be done. I hoped you would be sensible.'

There was no bargaining: she did not offer quid pro quo. She had come for a loan and it had been refused. That was the end of it – for her.

'Good-night, Mr Black.' She picked up her bag, stuffed the cheque inside and snapped the fastening.

'You're not in a hurry?' he asked.

She waited.

'The villa at Cannes – delightful! One can see you growing old there, an almost saintly figure. And in the Casino – a venerable and frugal gambler. Mr George Loamer would find it irksome, but he could travel.'

He showed all his teeth in a smile.

'There is a convict establishment at Aylesbury – for women! Have you ever thought of that as an unpleasant alternative to Cannes, Mrs Loamer! I went there once – line upon line of drab women in grey, walking in a circle and looking at the ground. The dead alive!'

II

Mrs Loamer did not blench: she raised her lorgnettes deliberately and examined him.

'Is that – er – a threat?'

'It is a possibility,' he said. 'I don't know ... you haven't made up my mind. I admire you tremendously – I admired you that night when I saw you were the managing director of the firm. Your courage is beyond praise. There is a tiny loophole for you – it is in Dover Harbour – the narrowish entrance to a pier where the cross-Channel steamer is waiting for the just and the unjust. Write off your bad debts, go abroad, and live on your jewellery.'

She walked in her stately fashion to the door.

'Good-night,' she said.

'Good-night – will you please not make a noise as you pass through the hall – Dr Elvington is very ill.'

She swung round.

'Elvington ... Dr Elvington?' harshly. 'What do you mean?'

'Very ill,' he murmured.

She looked up and down the parlour, a wondering frown on her forehead.

'Here?'

'He has just come back from hell,' said Robin. 'Ten years of it. Think of it, Mrs Loamer! Ten odd years of servitude in order that you should bedeck your ageing person with jewellery and pay fashionable pianists large fees! Ten years of being kicked and cuffed – and all because a clever lady wanted his money to fling into the gutter!'

He had pulled off the mask: she had lost self-control and looked pitiably old.

'You're lying. I would never have touched his money – '

She stopped suddenly.

'Did you know him?'

He saw from her expression that she did.

'The lady who opened the door to you is his daughter. You owe her a life, Mrs Loamer.'

Something in the old woman's face arrested his attention, and there began to dawn upon him a realisation that the story of Dr Marcus Elvington and his mysterious disappearance from the world had not been wholly told or wholly guessed. Was there more behind his reckless folly than had appeared? Some other explanation of his 'investment' than sheer lunacy? It was incredible, and yet –

'Where is he? I want to see him.'

Robin was dumbfounded.

'My dear good woman, you can't see him – '

'I want to see him!'

She threw open the door. On the other side of the hall she saw a light in the dining-room, but before she could cross the tiled floor Miss Ellen was in the doorway.

'Are you his daughter – Marcus Elvington's?' and, when Miss Ellen bowed: 'I am Mrs Loamer.'

Miss Ellen put out her hand to the wall for support. In the dim light of the little hall lamp Robin saw her face go whiter. October was in the background.

'I want to see your father ... is it true he is here?'

'Yes.' The word hardly reached the watchful man.

'Will you take me to him?'

Miss Ellen turned meekly to the stairs and led the way.

'Why is she seeing him?' October whispered.

'I don't know – I think I had better go up.'

He mounted the stairs two at a time and saw Mrs Loamer disappear into the doctor's room. The door was open; the old man lay on his back, looking strangely at the visitor. Miss Ellen folded her trembling hands, a picture of patience, of resignation, of sheer fatalism. In one corner of the room sat the aged maid, knitting on her lap, glooming over her steel-rimmed glasses at the visitor.

'Why, it's Julia!'

Julia! Robin nearly dropped with amazement. There was such affection, such yearning in the word.

Mrs Loamer was sitting on the bed, one of his hands

between hers. And in her dark eyes was such a look as Robin had never seen.

'Marky!'

Just that, in a husky, tear-choked voice. Robin swore softly to himself … he was dreaming surely.

' … why, Julia! Old "O" used to laugh at my Apparition … and here you are, darling! I always knew you'd come … do you remember that evening in Kensington, Julia … when I brought the money to you … '

He closed his eyes and seemed to be sleeping, but presently he spoke again.

'This, gentlemen, is a typical case of intracranial pressure. You will observe that the patient … '

His voice sank to a mumble, and when he spoke again it was of 'Julia' and 'money.'

Mrs Loamer did not speak; she sat with his hand in hers, her eyes roving the wasted face. What story was here, half told? – wondered Robin. He was never to know. Somewhere in the past of these two units of humanity was Romance … peculiar bonds not to be translated to his understanding. The souls of men and women are outside all measurement; their secret hearts defy comparison with formulae.

'Good to see you! Good to see you!'

The old man's voice was very clear. Five minutes passed without a sound … Only Robin knew that he was dead.

Mrs Loamer came downstairs, her head held high; there was no trace of emotion when she stood before Robin.

'I shall not see you again,' she said. 'Good-bye!'

He was mute. So much he might say, but all her barriers were up against speech. She hated him – hated him because he knew; hated him for what he was, for all that he represented.

She had concentrated upon him all the bitter malignity she felt towards a world that had suddenly grown bitter. He stood for one of the main obstacles that had baffled her throughout her life. It was war to the end. The knowledge set him tingling. He could have laughed as he stood on the top step and watched the car pull away into the night.

He closed the door and went into the parlour. October was

in her room – which was all to the good. He unfastened one of the shutters and pulled up the window. The drop to the terrace below was a gentle one. On the window sill he laid his electric torch that he had brought from October's room. Drawing the heavy cloth curtains across the window, he took out his automatic, stuffed two more cartridges in the magazine and another in the breech, pulled up the safety catch and dropped the weapon into his pocket. Amongst the articles he had asked Miss Ellen to buy for him was a dark raincoat – she had hung it in the hall. He found this, transferred the gun and hung the coat within reach.

The hall clock chimed one; it had the sound of a knell. Robin showed his teeth in a smile; it was his one gesture of defiance.

The handle of the door turned. It was October, and he had never seen her more depressed.

'It is dreadful. But, Robin, his poor daughter is wonderful – truly wonderful! That woman has gone?' He nodded. 'Isn't it ... unreal? And ugly!'

He nodded.

'It gave me the creeps – not the death of that poor old man. That was too natural to be anything but right. But she – sitting on the bed and holding his hand and all the ancient ghosts parading.'

'Tired?'

She shook her head.

'No – why?'

'We may have to leave in a hurry,' he said, and she nodded.

'I rather expected that – when?'

'I don't know. Soon, I think. I am only afraid of one thing, that they come "soft-footed to destroy." But that is hardly likely. We ought to hear the car in time.'

'The police?' She was startled.

'The police – the last refuge of the wicked. Gunmen do not grow on bushes or Julia – oh, what a name! – would pick a quart. I'm going out to sit on the doorstep.' He swept up his coat. 'Will you explain to Miss Ellen? And, October, get into everything that is new, and wait for me here.'

He opened the front door softly and went down to the gate. The world was silent and mysteriously without movement. His light suit made him conspicuous – he pulled on the coat and buttoned it to his neck; the sleeves were too long for effective gun-play – these he rolled back.

Not a sound ...

Ten minutes passed; the hall clock chimed the quarter. There appeared far away to his left two twinkling stars of light. Mrs Loamer's car, he guessed. The lights grew brighter; to his ears came the hum of the engines. How near would she come? Not much nearer apparently. The lights went out and the engines ceased to purr. The police car was noisier. He must hear this before he made a move.

There it was – a harsher moan. He walked back into the house and closed the door. Miss Ellen was in the parlour.

'Your wife has told me you are leaving – I made this ready for you.'

It was a packet of food; he thanked her and dropped it into his pocket.

'We must go through the window,' he said, and asked her to close and shutter it after them.

As October dropped to his side on the stone flags, he heard the police car distinctly.

'This way.'

He took her hand. October had not touched his hand since the night of her escape, she realised; it felt very strong and capable.

Through the tree belt, across the track garden into the meadow ... he helped her over the gap in the hedge. Somewhere a railway engine was coughing asthmatically.

He stooped and looked along the road. There was a grade here up which the express that carried poor Baldy might speed at forty miles an hour, but no heavy goods train would make that time.

Still holding hands, they made a cautious way along the ties. Presently they cleared the obstruction of the house and could see the tree-lined road. The police car had halted short of its objective. Men were tumbling out to the road. To go further was to show themselves against the skyline. The track ran along the top of an embankment; there was a little culvert ahead over a small stream. Better to wait, he thought, and sought a hiding place. There was a small pile of railway ties, and behind this they crouched.

'I don't know what this train is, but our only chance of escape this way is to find a closed truck with the doors open. If that fails us we must cross the rails and take to the fields.'

The train was near now; the light of its two headlamps lit the bushes and trees that fringed the track. And then it came into sight – a white beam shot along the metals.

'Wait till I say "Go",' he whispered. 'Don't try to climb – wait until I have boarded the truck.'

The engine grunted past ... October could see the train crew in the light of the furnace fire ... they were in darkness again. He touched her arm and she rose.

Truck after truck passed, and then:

'Follow!' he whispered and, running, reached up and caught a steel rod and hoisted himself through the open door of a van. Instantly he turned and, reaching down, gripped her wrist and pulled her up, breathless and triumphant.

Looking back in the direction of the house, he saw little lights flashing in Miss Ellen's garden – thought he saw a man running beside the track; but, since the train increased its speed as it reached the top of the grade and began the down-hill run, he thought he might be mistaken.

'We're here!' he said grimly.

'There is somebody in the car!' she whispered.

He took the torch from his pocket and flashed the light around. At the far end of the car lay two ragged man half-covered by straw. They were sleeping peacefully.

'Where are we going?'

It was the old question, and she nearly laughed at its familiarity.

'I don't know – London, I think. We are moving in that direction.'

The train whammed on at a pace which he likened to a steady jogtrot. Oncc, with a thundering rattle of buffer against buffer, they pulled up at a little station. Two men walked along the line, one of them swinging a lantern.

' ... found that man yet ... yes – murder! Killed another tramp – he orter get a medal for that!'

They were discussing tramps as they came back.

'Gow, two in here – look.'

He sent the light of his lantern towards the sleeping men. October squeezed herself tight against the wall. Robin had chosen the other end of the car, and the two men did not look in their direction. The lantern was withdrawn.

' ... what's the use? You throw 'em out and likely enough they wait for you one fine night and its "John Smith, aged thirty-eight. No flowers." Let 'em sleep.'

The train moved on for a few miles and then stopped. Looking out, Robin saw a man with a red lamp walking down the track towards the engine in the blinding light of the headlamp. He saw the glint of light on a helmet – a police officer!

He imparted the news to the girl.

'He's come on a motor-bicycle,' he surmised.

He pulled open the big door on the far side of the car and dropped to the line, and in another second she had joined him. There was no station building in sight, but a hundred yards in front of the engine he saw a level crossing. The cycle would be there – he almost imagined that he could see the light of it. They reached the sandy ditch by the side of the track and, leading the way, Robin crawled towards the head of the train. He could hear voices above the hiss of the escaping steam – a volley of questions and answers.

The sound of steam stopped suddenly.

' ... only one van that's empty – all the others are sealed ... two tramps, but I've had 'em since Ascot.'

Sound of heavy feet plodding along the track side. The engine crew were leaning out of the cab that they might miss nothing – their backs were towards the fugitives.

The danger was the nearside headlamp. It threw a beam that covered both rails; but the ditch became deeper, and by stooping they could keep their heads below its edge. Walking was difficult. They were tramping through mud; their feet became entangled with coarse water-grasses. Robin found a deep mud-hole and sank up to his knees.

'Farewell, new suit!' he groaned as he guided her past the trap. The crossing was a dozen yards away, and there was no sign of a motor-cycle. 'We can't expect everything,' said Robin philosophically, and at that second the rays of the headlamp were reflected dimly on polished steel. It was on the right side of the road, too – they need not cross the line.

He climbed up the steep bank, pullng her with him.

'You'd better lie down – '

Pang!

A bullet struck the wire fence on which his hand rested, and hummed into the night. The shot came from the ditch fifty yards behind them. October saw the flash.

III

'Run!'

She was on her knees, but he jerked her to her feet and, stooping, they flew.

Pang!

Robin stumbled forward – her heart stood still.

'Nothing – caught me a clip on the head, but nothing.'

He was under cover, tinkering furiously with the big motor-cycle.

'Give me the pistol.'

He handed it to her without a word, and she crept forward. A man was running along the track towards them, but her eyes were only for the hidden assassin in the ditch.

And then she saw him and fired. The force of the recoil startled her no less than the violence of the explosion. She felt her hand tingle hotly.

'Come!' It was Robin calling. He was straddling the machine, its headlamp burnt brilliantly. 'Up behind me on the carrier – hang on!'

She obeyed, found a steel grille at the back of the seat and sat sideways, her arms around his body. He kicked at the starter ... there was a splutter and bang, and they glided forward, gathering speed.

'Wow-w-w!'

'The policeman will stop him shooting in a minute,' shouted Robin. 'Don't worry ... rotten target!'

It seemed an eternity before the road crooked round and the railway was out of sight. She could see its reflected searchlight for a long time. The cycle behaved nobly; over his shoulder Robin shouted encomia of its sterling qualities. They met only one man, an elderly gentleman driving a trap, whose horse reared up and shied towards the side of the road. He hurled fierce imprecations after them.

'A doctor,' roared Robin. 'Only excuse for man his age being out late.'

The wind tore speech to fragments – they were moving at a rate which made conversation a matter of guesswork.

Apparently he had no route in his mind, but he told her afterwards that he was following a simple plan – first road to right – then first road to left.

'Red Beard – ditch!'

She gasped.

'The man who fired at us?'

'Jumped – train – same time – we. Thought – spotted him.'

He checked the speed of the machine, and after a few minutes stopped. She was not sorry to leave the carrier. It was of steel, in pattern rather like a grid. Robin put out the headlight.

'There will be a telephone within a mile of where the train stopped,' he said. 'By now the constabulary of the county will be looking for a lady and gentleman riding the wind.'

He picked up the machine and toppled it over a low wall into a field.

'We are approaching a town of some kind,' he said. 'Did you see the hotel advertisement in that field we just passed? Advertisements of hotels are the heralds of civilised communities.'

He stooped and with a stick scraped the drying mud from his trousers.

'You were about to ask where do we go from here?' he said.

'I wasn't!' she affirmed stoutly. 'I've ceased to be curious. I should like to know – '

'Where we are – so should I.' He put up his head and sniffed. 'Can't you smell it?'

'What?'

'Water – river, canal, something. I can smell it now. Glory be!'

She sniffed up the cool night air, but detected nothing that reminded her of anything.

'We're near the Thames,' he said seriously; 'how near or just where, I'm not troubling to think. I wonder where we can hide.'

They walked on and, as he had anticipated, came soon to a collection of houses. Their character and appearance were hidden. No wandering policeman was encountered, and they emerged into the country again in five minutes.

'The name of that thriving city might have helped us if we knew it,' he said. 'There was a shop that sold fishing-tackle: did you notice that?'

She hadn't, and marvelled that he could have made such a discovery in the darkness.

They stopped at the branch of the road and decided to take that which led to the left hand. It seemed the less cared for. It proved to be a cheerless way. A wind sprang up before dawn, and there was a nip in it that chilled his thinly covered legs.

' ... if I might mention anything so indelicate.'

He could mention anything without protest from October. Her own legs were aching; she had an overwhelming desire to sleep, and had he suggested that they should lie down in the middle of the road, she would have offered no objection.

The sky had clouded over, they saw, with the coming of the first grey light. On and on they trudged along the uneven road. Twice he stopped to let her rest – the second time he had to shake her awake. She was apologetic in a sleepy way and tried to be brightly conversational.

'An intensive education in cinema clichés tells me that you will turn out to be a secret service man who is flying from a gang of international war makers,' she said. 'You have the secret plans of – of the next war in your boot-heel – or maybe concealed in your vest; with a little card that you've only to show to the police to – to – '

'Get a cigar,' he humoured her. 'No, I'm nothing so romantic.'

'Then you're the heir to a great fortune that Lady Thingummy wants. You have a fleur de lys tattooed on your right arm.'

'Heir to the ages – no. The only person who ought to die and leave me something is Mrs Loamer. And I'll bet she won't. Try another.'

'I can't – I'm talking nonsense. You're Mr Tramp and I'm Mrs Tramp, and we'll wake up in the police station, and I shall be petted by the Society for the Protection of Lady Tramps.'

She scarcely realised that he had guided her from the main road, and that they were trudging through one of his favourite lanes.

She was sleeping on her feet, her arm linked in his, when she became conscious that they had stopped.

She stared stupidly at a narrow stream of black-looking water. Moored to the bank was a long black barge. There was light enough to see a man curled up on the bank under a gaily-coloured blanket. When they came up to him they saw he was black, and that his dazzling bedspread was only one of many. Nearby were the ashes of a fire. An old tin kettle blackened with much use, and a grub box. But neither kettle nor food were responsible for his deep and stertorous sleep.

Robin picked up the empty bottle and sniffed.

'Guaranteed to kill at fifty yards,' he said. 'Snowball has been enjoying a solitary jag.'

Between bank and barge was a plank; he walked aboard and looked round. The barge was empty – its usual cargo of coal, he saw. At one end in the stern was a hatchway which was unlocked. He made an inspection of the cramped quarters. Apparently this was the sleeping and living room of the crew.

In the bow was a small compartment with a wooden bunk but having no evidence of occupation. It was approached through a sliding hatch, but the hasp by which the door was fastened had been broken off.

He returned to find October sitting on the bank, her arms folded on her knees, her head on her arms. Lifting her bodily, he carried her across the plank, which sagged under them so that the yard of their progess required an extraordinary effort, and eventually got her into the close little cubby hole. Laying her on the bunk with his rolled coat under her head, he pushed the door tight and stretched himself on the floor, and fell into a painful sleep. In his dreams he heard voices shouting anathemas upon the heads of all boozing niggers, the slow drag of feet, and a guttural, whining voice raised in exculpation.

Thump!

A heavy object fell on the deck above his head. He stared round, saw that October had rolled perilously near to the edge of the bunk and pushed her back unceremoniously with his foot, before he fell off to sleep again.

He woke with a taste of tar in his mouth, and saw that October was sitting on the edge of the bunk eating a biscuit. Her face was black.

'There was a letter for you,' she said, and handed down an envelope.

'Has the post come?'

There was no light to read; he slipped it into his pocket.

'It was wrapped up with the food,' said October. 'Isn't everything quiet? You look funny!'

She began to laugh, quietly at first, and then mirth shook her.

'If it is the coal dust on my face that amuses you,' he said, 'perhaps you would like to see your own.'

She had a bag and a mirror. Her exclamation of horror was pleasant hearing. He opened the hatch a little and peeped cautiously out. The banks were travelling past – the barge was on the move. Looking aft, he saw the negro sitting with a blanket about his shoulders, his head on his breast, one hand on the long tiller. He pulled open the hatch a little farther, got his head and shoulders out. Ahead of them was a little tug boat, and between barge and tug a hawser slapped up and down in the water.

He went down to the girl, but the cabin was empty – a mystery explained when she crawled out through the narrowest door he had ever seen. There was a wash-place there with a rusty little pump that yielded a trickle of water.

'Which way are we going?' she asked in alarm.

'That way,' he pointed. 'Whether it leads to London or – wherever canals lead, I don't know. We must lie low until night.'

He closed the door and, visiting the wash-room, succeeded in removing some of the grime from his face. With the hatch closed, the atmosphere was stuffy. October developed a headache and went to sleep again. Every hour or so Robin took an observation. Once, when he looked out, the barge was under the shadow of a wharf, and he saw the smoke of locomotives.

It must have been four o'clock when the tug ceased to haul. The bump of the barge as it struck the bank awakened the girl. Robin went to his peep-hole.

'We are taking more barges in tow.'

After the exchange of a considerable quantity of bad language between the captain of the tug and the negro at the tiller, in which the skipper was aided and abetted by an unknown called 'Tom', who evidently was posted on the canal bank, progress was resumed. Robin dozed, and dreamt that he was back in the Shepherd's house and could not leave it because before every door and window swung the body of the departed owner. He felt a pressure on his arm and woke.

'We have stopped,' she whispered in his ear. 'I heard somebody ask the negro if he had seen a man and a woman when he stopped last night.'

Feet sounded on the deck – booted, heavy feet.

'What's down here?'

The door to the washroom was a thick plank, opening on hinges inwards. Robin gathered up his coat and the girl's hat and bag and pushed her through the opening. He followed and, bracing his feet against the barge's timbers, set his back firmly against the door. He heard the hatch grind back and heavy feet tread the floor of the bunkhouse.

'Nobody hear, sah. I bin in dis cabin an' outer dis cab'n all day, sah.'

'Where do you sleep?' asked an authoritative voice.

'Me, sah? I sleep up forrard, sah. There ain't nothin' in my cab'n, sah!'

There was a crash as the hatch closed, and they were gone. Robin stole out and listened, heard later an angry colloquy. After that an animated and interminable conversation went on somewhere near, but Robin could hear nothing. The barge must be tied up to some wharf, for he heard the rumble of wagon wheels and the slow clip-clop of a horse's hooves. The talkers were moving in his direction. Robin heard authority again.

' ... now look here, Byrne – '

Byrne! Robin dared move the hatch; the failing light justified the act.

' ... there's no argument. You get back to London and report to Scotland Yard. I've had orders to send you there ... I don't care what you're doing. I know, I *know*! We'll get the tramp without any assistance from you – thank you! I know just all about it ... '

Robin did not catch Red Beard's retort.

'Always glad of information, Mr Byrne. You traced him to the barge, did you ... I know all about the officer losing his machine. Well, he's not on the barge and never came on ... '

'Can't I stay the night? I'll go to London first thing in the morning. Listen, chief – this bird got my partner – right through the leg. I'm sore's hell. And this man is on the barge – him an' his chicken. He's somewheres round. I gotta instinct. Say, I'd give a million dollars to get him for you ... '

They were walking slowly as he spoke. Robin did not hear the reply. More deadly than all the detectives was Red Beard, for he had sources of information denied to the police. And he had the use of a fast car, could pick up the distinctive track of the cycle. It was not very hard to understand how this blood-hound came to nose along the trail. They had seen nobody on the journey except the old man in the trap. Who had seen them? What homeless men had looked out from their sleeping places and watched them pass in the light of dawn?

'There is nothing to do but wait,' he said.

October thought that he sounded rather middle-aged, and told him as much.

'Maybe; I feel a hundred. I don't know where we are, and we may blunder from the barge into the arms of a policeman.'

There was a church clock near them. They counted the quarters until ten struck. Robin opened the hatch and closed it again quickly. Two men were standing at the far end of the boat, visible in a distant arc-lamp. The negro was one, the other he recognised, though his back was turned. So Red Beard was back. That instinct of which he boasted had brought him. He was illustrating his words with his hands. He pointed down, he pointed first to one side of the barge and then the other, and then he turned round, and it was the negro who pointed. And a negro's gestures are expressive. By the slope of his hands Robin saw that he was indicating the cubby hole, then he pulled open an invisible plank and vigorously washed his face – pointed again. Red Beard was nodding. The negro took a step towards the fore cabin – Red Beard caught him by the arm and told him something ... all these events Robin repeated to the girl.

' ... the negro is firing a gun – Reddy has told him I am armed – Reddy is flapping his hand up and down as if he was saying "Leave him to me." Now he is leaving the barge – no, he isn't; he's going down to Snowball's dug-out – '

'Reddy fades out picture!' she said wearily. 'It sounds like an over-elaborated film scenario – '

Somebody called 'Bud' in a loud voice, and the negro came flying up to the deck – alone. He ran towards the hatch. Robin closed it quickly, and just then there was a thud on the deck. The barge bumped so violently that October was nearly thrown from her feet.

'We're on the move!' said Robin suddenly.

He could hear the panting of the tug – the barge lurched sideways. From the pier a man roared a string of rapid instructions, only the last four words of which could be distinguished.

'Don't forget the bacon.'

Evidently this was a time-honoured jest. The negro's roar of laughter filled all space.

'Ha, ha,' said Robin politely.

He was sitting by her side and, reaching out, took her hand.

'How did you know I wanted comfort?' she asked.

'Do you? Yes, I knew that. I am psychic. You have a forlornless.'

He heard her deep sigh and grinned.

'Don't laugh – I'm psychic, too!' she said fretfully. 'And I *know* you smiled. Do you realise that a week ago I had never slept in a haunted house, or in a barge, or ridden in a milk van with tramps, or seen anybody die? And it's ... well, crowding on me! And I feel that I'm going through life running away from something – the kind of nightmare you have after a bad supper – running away from a man with a knife, running, running, running until you wake up and turn on the light! Shall I wake up?'

'Yes, and you won't need to turn on the light – there will be sunshine and flowers and fountains playing and a brass band – everything the heart can desire.'

She drew a long breath.

'I don't see that – only horrid roads, and old sheds and goods trains ... tramps without end, hobbling along and to nowhere!'

He dropped her hand suddenly.

'Why?' she asked.

'You're shaking my nerve – and you mustn't do it, October.' His voice was almost sharp. 'I get panicky when you talk that way – when you feel that way. I just want to leap up on deck and shoot somebody – anybody. It is hysteria. Dash your auburn tresses, you've made me hysterical.'

'My hair isn't auburn,' she said coldly, and then laughed and squeezed his arm tight. 'I'm mean! I think I was depressed about Red Beard – I did so hope I had killed him! And then we could have sat side by side in court and cheered one another – the prisoner always gets the best seat in court.'

He laughed at this, rather more loudly than was safe ... overhead he heard the creak of a shoe and put his hand to her mouth.

'I wonder if he heard!'

Ten thousand pounds are a lot of pounds, as Red Beard often said to Lenny. And Lenny had invariably replied, 'Thasso!' A few minutes afterwards, he would grin from ear to ear, for he was a slow thinker, though an excellent judge of pace.

Red Beard squatted by the negro steersman, a cigar between his teeth, his arms clasped about his knees, and tried to imagine what they would look like – a hundred notes for a hundred pounds each, all spread out on a large table. It would have to be an enormously large table.

He watched the dark country pass on either bank, his eyes glued on the chuffing tug. The barge had passed out of the canal and was keeping to the central channel of the river that alternately sprawled and closed upon them. She – if a barge be not a neutral thing – was due to meet the *William and Mary*, a collier out of Cardiff, in the Pool of London, and Red Beard anticipated no more than a pleasant trip and a few quiet hours to exercise his thoughts. And the most pleasant of these was that ten thousand pounds are a lot of pounds.

Now suppose ...

The worst of men have their dreams, and they are usually about money.

Now suppose he had got that walking guy at Boulogne, or when he was leaning on the gate taking the air ... The thought thrilled him. Suppose he were on this very barge? Red Beard, though no Catholic, carried in his pocket a tiny silver medallion of St Anthony, reputedly a great help in finding articles you mislay. He possessed all the superstitions of his illiteracy, and in a grip now safely deposited in New York, at the Grand Central Station, he stored innumerable charms, which were all cunningly promoted and degraded as their potency failed. But St Anthony was one of the constants of his faith.

He took it out now, rubbed it on the palm of both hands, and deposited it religiously in the deeps of his pocket. This nigger talked of a recess opening from the forward cubby hole. It was queer finding a nigger bargee in England. ... But niggers are born liars and imagine things; and anyway, Red Beard had not thought it necessary to pursue his search. A thought occurred to him.

'Bud, go along and see what's down that hatch. I'll take your steering stick.'

'Me, sah? No, sah!' Bud shook his head vigorously. 'Dat place is ha'nted! Old man died down thah last time we was on the Surrey Canal.'

Red Beard tried to jeer him into making the investigation, but the man was adamant. He said that the night after the old man was moved the hatch was padlocked. Next morning the lock was broken. Another padlock was fixed and again was broken. According to him, this happened six nights out of seven. He did not explain that the only time it happened was when a shore thief came aboard in his absence, looking for loot. But Red Beard was impressed. He believed in ghosts and premonitions – pictures falling from the wall, and death tappings ...

He stared forward into the darkness apprehensively, but after a while he mastered his uneasiness, and walked along the narrow side deck, standing irresolutely above the hatch. And then he heard the laugh, and his heart leapt. Going down on his knees, he examined the covering. A broken staple gave support to the negro's legend, but Mr Byrne was superior now to superstitious fears. His fingers went gingerly along the slide. The hatch must be pushed towards the bow of the boat. If the staple were there, it would be easy enough to fasten. How else might it be kept closed? His practical mind found a way, and he went cautiously back to the uneasy steersman.

'Got an iron bar – anything!'

Bud, perturbed and frightened, went reluctantly down into his sleeping hole. In a box under the bunk were kept the ship's tools, a rusty collection of of axes, hammers and chisels. From the bottom Red Beard raked out two crowbars of different length and, armed with these, he went forward again. If the longer of the two bars had been made for the purpose, it could not have suited him better. With the claw fixed to the back of the hatch he hammered down the head of the crowbar against the prow post. Robin heard the hammering and, guessing its meaning, jumped for the hatch; he tried to pull it back, but not an inch would it yield.

'Put your hands to your ears,' he whispered.

And then, from the deck above, he heard a hateful voice.

'Hullo!'

Red Beard lay flat on the hatch and formed a trumpet of his two hands.

'Think you'll make London this trip? Like hell you will – '

Right at his elbow the wood splintered and flew upward. A second bullet snicked the tip of his ear … his face was smarting in a dozen places where the splinters had struck.

He scrambled to his feet with a bellow of rage and whipped out his gun. Ahead of them was a broad expanse of water, and as Red Beard fired, the tug was caught by the swift water of the river and swung round. From the little steamer's deck the skipper was shouting at him excitedly; the syren wailed; but Red Beard neither heard nor realised. Half-mad with rage, he danced up and down the little deck, his gun whirling.

'I'll fix you … I'll fix you!'

Again the pistol banged, but by now Robin had taken cover with the girl behind the stout plank.

Back to the stern and the alarmed Bud the gunman raced, vanished into the little cabin. The steersman heard the rattle and crash of the tool-box being overturned, and then the half-demented man came out carrying a rusty axe.

'Boss, fo' de Lawd's sake, what you gwine ter do? Boss, I'll get fired for dis sure … !'

But Red Beard swept him aside. The tug was panting against the stream; the hawser that held the barge was taut. With two blows he severed the rope, and without pause dropped down into the broad flat bottom of the barge. Crash! The axe fell on the floor, and as he lugged it back, a thin plank came up, revealing the black ribs and a layer of black water that covered the outer skin of this decrepit craft.

The negro was dancing to and fro, working the tiller first this way and that in his frenzy as the barge drifted in circles to the centre of the stream. The axe was useless – the bilge water was too deep. Red Beard clambered up to the foredeck and searched for the short crowbar, found it and, returning down, drove through the water to the bottom of the boat.

Red Beard's back straightened and his gun drove out.

'Stay where you are, nigger!'

'Fo' Gawd's sake, boss ... I cain't swim.'

'Get back – quick!' He fired a shot at the negro's foot and Bud clambered out of the well with a wild howl.

The wood was old and soggy: every blow of the sharp claw dug deeply into its rottenness. Panting, blinded with the perspiration which ran down his face at his unusual exertion, Red Beard drove down the bar and felt it slip through. Water bubbled up noisily; he struck again, broke off the edges of the hole he had made ... the river was above his ankles when he climbed to the after-deck.

He pushed the petrified steersman aside, dragging back the tiller so that the barge headed for the shore. It lurched sideways, turning round and round, now stern first, now broadside to the stream, but all the time edging towards the dark shore. In the well the water was rising slowly, bringing with it the loose deck boards that had covered its floor.

'I cain't swim, I cain't swim!' sobbed Bud.

'Shut up!' snapped Red Beard savagely. 'When we hit the bank, jump!'

Nearer and nearer to the shore the ungainly craft circled. She was so heavily waterlogged that she no longer responded to the rudder. Red Beard made a mental calculation and guessed that, by now, the people in the fore cabin had water up to their waists. Another and a stronger eddy caught them and brought the stern of the scow within a few feet of the bank. He had judged well ... there was a grinding thump and, with a scream of terror, Bud shot through the air like something released from a catapult, tumbled on to the steep bank and, by a superhuman effort, dragged himself to land.

Red Beard's departure was more dignified. He literally stepped from the rudder top to earth, and, save for wet feet, suffered no inconvenience.

The barge was drifting out again and, as it drifted, sank lower and lower till only the rims of the stern and bow showed. Presently it passed out of sight. Red Beard put up his hand to his lacerated cheek, drew out a splinter with a grimace and grinned.

'Figured I'd fix him, and I've fixed him!' he said complacently, and sat down to recover his breath and to debate in his mind the important question – was Lenny entitled to his agreed share of the blood-money?

'Fifty-fifty's all wrong,' said Red Beard.

The first intimation of danger that came to the two people in the cabin was a gushing of water through the loosely set floor-boards. At first Robin could not believe his eyes, and then, as there reached him the thud-thud of the falling crowbar and the gurgle of the inrushing water, the horror of the thing turned him cold.

With the help of his lamp, he made a hurried search for some means to break open the hatch. The plank that formed the door to the wash-room seemed the only possible instrument, but the hinges were tightly screwed, and not all his efforts could wrench one loose.

'We're sinking, aren't we?' asked October quietly.

'It feels that way,' he said.

'Is the knife any good?' she asked, and produced unexpectedly from her pocket the weapon that Lenny that thrown.

It was a clasp-knife of peculiar pattern: the blade, as long again as the handle, folded over, its edge being protected by a narrow steel groove which, when the knife was in use, fitted into the handle. He seized this timely weapon from her hand and, snapping it straight, attacked the hatchway. But the wood here was at least three-quarters of an inch thick, and although he had the advantage of working from the punctures which the bullets had made, there was little hope of cutting away sufficient to allow them to escape.

By now, as Red Beard had calculated, the water was between waist and armpits, and the barge was wallowing first to one side and then to the other, and with every drunken stagger of it they thought the end had come.

'Will the hatch slide in the other direction?' she asked.

He examined the edge and saw at once that the wooden cover was kept in its place by a flimsy strip of wood, which was already strained and bent under the pressure of the hammered crowbar. Driving the knife into the wood, he had the satisfaction of tearing off a long splinter without trouble. A second slither followed. As he struck again he heard the bump of the stern as it struck the bank. The water was now up to his shoulders and he worked at fever speed, handicapped by the presence of the girl, whom he had been forced to put in front of him on the lower of the three steps that led down from the deck. He pried loose yet another jagged slip and, planting his hands on the under side of the hatch, exerted all his strength and pushed. The hatch did not open, as he expected; it gave half-an-inch and then stuck. But that half-an-inch produced a result he had not anticipated. The iron bar fell to the deck with a clang and, reversing the motion of his hands, he pulled and the hatch slid back. Linking his arm in hers, he dragged her to the deck, already under water.

'Can you swim, October?'

'Yes ... how far and for how long?'

It seemed there was no need to swim for any distance. As the craft careened round, out of the darkness on their left loomed a low bank. In another instant they were in the water, swimming strongly against the current. Then, reaching out his hand, Robin dug his fingers into a clay bank and they slipped and slid up its steep and oozy face until his hand touched the thorny branches of a bush.

October was the first to recover her speech.

'*Now* where are we?' she asked.

'I'm damn'd if I know!' said Robin, 'but I'm in favour of a tax on betting!'

It was the first time he had used strong language in her presence, and in the circumstances she felt that he was justified.

Presently he gripped her hand and lifted her.

'Walk,' he said. 'You'll be chilled to death sitting there in those wet clothes. We'll find a house somewhere.'

They struggled through the bramble of a little wood and emerged on the other side, to find there was a broad canal to cross. Along this they wandered until they came to a deserted lock, which gave them a bridge. Before them at the foot of a long hill they saw the lights of a considerable town. Presently, labouring across the field, they found a road.

'Once more we take to the broad highway,' said October gaily; 'and if this is Ashleigh I shall scream!'

'It is anywhere but Ashleigh,' he said, 'but I thought I recognised ... no, I didn't! But I've been in this town before.'

He felt in his pocket and his hand touched the sodden roll of notes he had taken from Lenny – who was the cashier of the confederation.

'We'll go straight to the best hotel,' he said firmly, 'order a hot dinner and a hot bath.'

Somebody was walking ahead of them – a stranger like themselves, for, hearing footsteps behind him, he stopped and turned.

'Say, mister, what place is this? I just landed from a barge – '

It was Red Beard. Robin slipped his arms from his wet jacket.

'This is the place you get off, whiskers!' he said, and drove with his left.

Red Beard fell with a crash, but in a second he was on his feet and had jerked out his gun. Before he could rise it, a hand gripped his wrist and twisted it so painfully that with a yell the gunman dropped his weapon. It fell at October's feet and she kicked it to the side of the road.

Red Beard was game, but he was no hand fighter. The third time he went down he elected to stay. Robin searched round for the pistol, put it in his pocket and walked back to his enemy.

'Are you insured, Byrne?' he asked. 'Because, if you are, I'm entitled to a commission from the company that took the risk. Ninety-nine cents to the dollar is your premium if you and I ever meet again! Do you get that?'

Red Beard did not answer. He was counting his teeth.

The end of the road brought them to the beginning of a street.

'We shall attract a little attention, October, but I can't risk your running round in damp clothes.'

The town was peculiarly constructed: it consisted of one main avenue with practically no houses behind on either side, and a large proportion of the buildings were devoted to the rest and freshment of man. There was a festive gaiety about the place which seemed more unreal to October, who knew the river, than to her companion. It was one of those little bungalow communities which are desolations in the late autumn. A group of cottages, two little hotels, and a line of closed boat-houses, suggested that the community enjoyed only a seasonal prosperity.

The chill wind that swept down the long street was responsible for its deserted appearance – they did not see even a policeman, though there was a knot of people about the enticing and brightly illuminated entrance of the inevitable cinema.

'The best hotel is any hotel,' said Robin, 'and this place looks good to me.'

It was a two-storey house standing back from the road behind a grassy forecourt, and the open hallway, with its gaily coloured lights, decided him. Across the broad fanlight were the words 'River Hotel,' and as they stepped into the warm vestibule a heavenly smell of cooking food came out to meet them.

Robin searched for a bell and found it, and presently a stout little woman, with huge, gold-rimmed spectacles, appeared with the set smile of one who had profited by her contact with humanity. The smile faded at the sight of the two coal-stained and bedraggled scarecrows. Robin hastened to remove the unfavourable impressions which they had created.

'We've been picnicking on a barge,' he said, 'but

unfortunately we didn't choose a clean one, and we finished up our trip by falling into the water. Can you let us rooms?'

'Why – yes,' she hesitated, and then, with an 'Excuse me,' she darted through a door and returned immediately with a large red-haired man chewing a toothpick, who surveyed them solemnly, critically and appraisingly.

'Well,' he drawled, when he had found his voice, 'I don't know that this hotel will suit you. Maybe if you go along to Mrs Hodges – she's open all the winter.'

'We're closing down to-morrow,' jerked in the stout little woman. 'All our boarders are gone and we have no staff.'

'We only want rooms for the night,' said Robin.

The big man chewed his toothpick with his eye on his wife, and Robin thought it a good moment to produce from his unpleasantly damp pocket a mass of wet paper.

'I'd like you to dry this for me,' he said, and at the sight of so much indubitably good money the big man was galvanised into a violent interest.

'Of course I will,' he said. 'You count it out, because I don't want any argument after. Mother, you'll find a room for this gentleman and lady. Married?'

Robin parried.

'Two rooms,' he said soberly, 'and if possible, two bathrooms.'

'We've got three,' said the proprietor, with some pride.

He came up to collect the money and told Robin that they were the only guests in the house. Apparently they shut down at the end of August, but the September had been so unusually fine that a number of the bungalows in the town had dragged out their period of occupation.

'You'll be wanting some more clothes,' said the big man. 'Would you like me to 'phone up to Sturgess and ask them to send you some down? Perhaps your wife would like something dry?'

It was an excellent scheme. Robin was hardly out of a scalding hot bath when Mr Sturgess himself, happy to find customers at this dead-end of the season, arrived with two big suitcases.

They dined in solitary-state, he and October, in a large, over-ornamented dining-room, economically darkened except for a lamp over their table.

They had retired to the hotel parlour, there to discuss the morrow, when the first hint of trouble came. Next to the parlour was the proprietor's office, and only a thin matchboarding separated the two rooms. Robin had heard the telephone bell ring before, and had been an unwilling eavesdropper to conversation which consisted of the unimportant exchanges of intimate gossip that make up the life of a small community.

Mr Sturgess, who had brought the clothes, had told him that they were twelve miles from London.

'In which direction?' asked October.

'I didn't ask him that. He was a very short-speech little man. I've never met a salesman who spoke less.'

He was rising to search for a newspaper when he heard the telephone bell ring and the proprietor's voice answer.

'Hey? ... Yes, inspector ... ' A long pause. 'Yes, two people ... that's right, a man and a woman. Wait a minute.'

He got up and closed the door of his office, rather unnecessarily, as it happened.

'Yes, about an hour ago ... ' Another pause, and then, in a tone of consternation: 'You don't mean that!'

And then the receiver was hung up.

They looked at one another.

'The Great Highway, I think,' said Robin carefully, and at that moment the proprietor came in and closed the door behind him. In his hand he had a half-dried sheaf of notes.

'You'd better take these – and get out.'

'I haven't paid my bill,' said Robin.

'Don't worry about that. Killed a tramp, did you?'

He shook his head in wonder. Robin had the idea that the gesture held not a little admiration, too.

He personally conducted them on to the roadway.

'They'll come from the left. You had best go right till you come to the London Road.'

Robin shrank back to cover as a car came speeding up the street and stopped before the door. Three men jumped out. In point of fact, only two should have alighted: the driver's place was at the wheel, but he was curious, and curiosity has been the ruin of more men than women. He had hardly joined the group at the boarding-house door before he saw the car moving ...

'They must have slipped down the side path – ' began the proprietor, but nobody waited to hear him.

V

Mr George Loamer strutted across the wide stretch of the outer office, beamed benevolently upon an intimate secretary, and passed into his own room. There was no evidence of perturbation or distress. He was his immaculate self, and hung his polished silk hat upon a peg with the greatest of care before he seated himself in his comfortable chair, glanced at the mass of unopened letters which awaited him, and rang a bell. His secretary came in.

'Dowdlers have been three times about their account – ' he began, but Mr Loamer silenced him good-humouredly.

'I have to go to Paris this afternoon,' he said, took a cheque from his waistcoat pocket and smoothed it out flat upon the blotting-pad.

The secretary took it up, glanced at the figure and his mouth opened wide.

'You want all this in cash, Mr Loamer?' he asked in a hushed voice.

Mr Loamer nodded.

'Take a cab, and when you've drawn the money go to the Bank Lyonnaise and change it into francs.'

He locked the door after the man had gone, opened an intricate little wall safe that was concealed behind the panelling, took out a small account book, a number of papers, and carried them to the fireplace. From his hip pocket he took a whisky flask, sprinkled its contents upon the papers, and the pungent scent of petrol filled the office. Mr Loamer struck a match and watched the blaze complacently, turning over the slower burning account book with a poker. Not until the handsome grate was filled with black ashes did he withdraw his gaze.

The panelled wall also concealed a cupboard, and from this Mr Loamer took out a flat suitcase and, putting it on his desk, unlocked the door and rang again. This time one of the girl clerks answered him.

'Send the commissionaire to me.'

The commissionaire came, a grizzled man with two rows of war ribbons.

'Take this to Victoria Station and wait until I come,' he instructed, and the man carried the bag out.

There was a smaller bag, but this Mr Loamer decided to carry himself.

Again he explored the cuboard, brought out a rough tweed suit and, locking the door, made a quick change. He tidied away the clothes he had discarded, took a cardboard box from the smaller bag, and in a paper covering found the wig which had been made for him a year before, and the bristling iron-grey moustache which the finest costumier in London had assured him would defy detection under the eyes of experts. That disguise could be very quickly effected after he had met the commissionaire at the railway station.

He snapped the bag tight, unlocked the door, and sat down patiently to await the return of his messenger. He was an unconscionable time. Mr Loamer grew impatient, a little apprehensive, but presently through the sliding panel he saw the man walking back quickly, and heard him enter before he tapped at the door. One glance at the secretary's face told him the worst.

'The bank wouldn't honour the cheque, sir. I told them I knew you had the balance, but they said they wanted to see you first. The clerk said that they'd had a wire from somebody.'

Not a muscle of George Loamer's face moved.

'That is very foolish of them. Thank you, Carter, I will see the manager myself.'

When the man had gone, he searched the inside of his waistcoat pocket. There was a thick wad of notes there, sufficient to get him away and maintain him for two years; but it would have been better if he could have taken the bank balance. He did not think of his mother; he dared not think of her. The lifetime habit of obedience and servitude was not easily to be broken.

Pulling open a drawer of his desk, he unlocked a little cash-box which he had regarded as too insignificant to investigate, but every pound counted now.

He had emptied the box when there came a tap at the door. Mr Loamer hesitated for a moment.

'Come in,' he said, and there walked into the office a very bronzed, good-looking young man, who greeted him with a nod and a smile.

'Good-morning, Mr Loamer – you owe me five thousand pounds.'

Mr Loamer's face was a picture of surprise and pleasure.

'My dear Mr Black!' he said. 'When did you get back?'

Nigel Black pulled up a chair and sat down, in such a position that he was between Mr Loamer and all possibility of escape.

'I arrived in town at five o'clock this morning,' he said grimly, and Mr Loamer beamed.

'You shall have a cheque at once, my dear fellow,' he said, found his cheque book and spoke as he wrote. 'An achievement – a wonderful achievement! Upon my word, I never would have imagined that you would ever win your wager! I don't suppose there's another man in England who has walked to Paris and back, starting out without a shilling – '

'A cheque isn't much use, Mr Loamer. The police have instructed your bankers not to honour your signature.'

Even this did not ruffle the placidity of one who had been regarded as a pillar of finance.

'You don't really mean that? What an extraordinary thing to happen! Ha, ha, that's rather a good joke.'

'I will do all the laughing that's necessary,' said Nigel Black. 'I haven't been to the bank, so I am still in ignorance as to the fate of my million dollars – I presume that can be wiped out?'

'Your million dollars,' said Loamer pleasantly, 'is quite intact. You will forgive me, Mr Black, if I say that I think your manner is a little strange and wild. Americans, as I know to my cost, are eccentric, but I confess I have never met anybody as eccentric as you. I owe you five thousand pounds and I am willing to pay it. You have won your bet, and it is a lesson to me never to take uncommercial risks. Betting is a practice which I cannot too strongly deprecate – '

'Your mother was arrested this morning – an hour ago,' said Nigel quietly, and George Loamer's face went grey. 'When she was arrested,' continued the young man, 'she did not preserve the calm which is so admirable in you. In fact, Mr Loamer, she was very talkative.'

The big man sat numb, incapable of speech; despair in his eyes, his plump hands twitching convulsively.

'She told Mr Simpson, who is an officer at Scotland Yard, and who will be along here presently, quite a number of queer stories. For example, she said that this business was started on borrowed money and kept in being by systematic fraud and – murder.'

Loamer blinked at this, but gave no other sign.

'She was very frank about her own innocence,' Nigel went on, 'and I should imagine will be the principal witness at your trial; but she complained bitterly of the stupidity which brought her to her present unhappy position – your stupidity.'

'Oh, did she?' muttered Loamer.

'It was a queer, horrible story of people who had trusted you with their money – and disappeared. Or, if they did not disappear, died suddenly. October Jones does not know, and never will know, the cause of her mother's death. Poor old Elvington cannot tell us of other wretched creatures who had been kept at Four Beeches long after their money was dissipated and they were forgotten; but the police have traced from local records the death of at least three men and one woman who went to Four Beeches and never returned to the world.'

'They died naturally,' murmured Mr Loamer.

'That we shall discover,' said Nigel sternly.

George Loamer staggered to his feet, stood for a moment, his big hands on the desk supporting his weight, and then with unsteady footsteps walked to a corner of the room and stood with his back to the man he had designed for death.

'I'm not complaining about my mother ... I'm saying nothing ... If she says I am to blame, I *am* to blame.'

His sensitive ears heard quick, precise footsteps on the floor outside. He bent his head listening and then his hand went up to his forehead in a gesture of weariness and there was a sharp explosion.

Before Nigel could reach him he had sunk in a huddled heap in the corner of the room.

'So far as I can discover,' said Nigel Black, when he called at October's hotel a fortnight later, 'your fortune is, with the exception of a few thousand pounds, very much as it ought to be. Loamer had not had time to make the transfer, though if he'd had another few weeks I think your money would have gone the way of others.'

'Poor souls!' She looked at him. 'And you?' she asked and shook her head. 'You've lost yours, of course?'

'Less than half of it,' he said cheerfully, 'but a half is more than I ever expected to recover.'

They had taken Mrs Loamer that morning to a mental institution.

'Where she should have been forty years ago. She's undoubtedly mad.'

'Did she know about – ' The girl hesitated.

'About her son's suicide? Oh, yes, she discussed it quite calmly. She even said that it was the best thing that could possibly have happened.'

His arm slipped round October's shoulder and he put one hand under her chin and raised her face to his.

'We're going to be married in three days, October Jones – a real marriage this time. And I've a perfectly wonderful idea for a honeymoon.'

She looked at him suspiciously.

'We'll go a walking tour through – '

'No!' said October Jones, very decidedly.